AF560641

CIVIL SOCIETY AND HEALTH

CIVIL SOCIETY AND HEALTH

Edited by

Mr. Manas Ranjan Pradhan
Mr. Aditya Kumar Patra
Mr. Rajib Lochan Panigrahy

DISCOVERY PUBLISHING HOUSE PVT. LTD.
NEW DELHI-110 002

Published by:
Tilak Wasan

DISCOVERY PUBLISHING HOUSE PVT. LTD.
4383/4B, Ansari Road, Darya Ganj
New Delhi-110 002 (India)
Phone : +91-11-23279245, 43596064-65
Fax : +91-11-23253475
E-mail : parul.wasan@gmail.com
discoverypublishinghouse@gmail.com
web : www.discoverypublishinggroup.com

***First Edition:* 2012**

ISBN: 978-93-5056-068-6

Civil Society and Health

Printed at:
Shree Balaji Art Press
Delhi

Preface

"Health is Wealth". Good Health and environment is the right of a citizen of a country or organization. It is a very popular notation in the society. In any economy, the people living in the nation or organization is the asset which is called as resources of factors of production. If the human resources are healthy, the economy will be healthier. So, the nation in which people are living or organization where the people are working has its duty to maintain the healthy society within it.

More governance is required for proper health of the population with social atmosphere giving proper weightage to the public health both physical and mental. Government have assignments on health, sanitation, environment. In the highly populated country such as India, most of the people are living in villages and many are living in slums, etc. Though who are living in urban areas, they are also living in less hygienic conditions, polluted environments.

Most health matters of India in such an over crowdedness and rapid population growth, the researchers has been contributed their valuable unique research articles to this book which compiles it a healthier one. So, we congratulate for their article(s) and owe out sense of gratitude for their timely contribution. Again we are very much thankful to the publisher to make it success to see the limelight.

Hope, it will be helpful to the authors, researchers, readers, libraries.

Editors

Contents

List of Contributors

1. **Mr. Sateesh Gouda M** is part time Research Scholar in GUG and has been working as Monitoring and Evaluation Specialist in KHPT Bellary, Karnataka.

   Dr. A.G. Khan is Reader and Head in Dept of Sociology, Government Degree Collage, Aland, Gulbarga, Karnataka.

2. **Manas Ranjan Pradhan**, PhD, Senior Programme Specialist, Futures Group International, DLF Building No 10-B, 5th Floor, DLF Cyber City, Phase-II, Gurgaon-122 002, India

3. **Dr. Chander Shekhar**, Associate Professor, IIPS, Mumbai

   Binod Bihari Jena, Research Scholar, JNU, New Delhi

4. **Sandhya Rani Mahapatro**, Research Scholar (Population Research Center), Bangalore, India

5. **Ravi Prakash**, Karnataka Health Promotion Trust (KHPT), Bangalore-560044

   Praveen Kumar Pathak, Senior Research Fellow, International Institute for Population Sciences (IIPS), Mumbai-400088

6. **Sangram Panigrahi**, Junior Research Fellow at Gokhale Institute of Politics and Economics, Pune-411004

7. **Skylab Sahu**
8. **Kaveesher Krishnan**, Ph.D Fellow, Centre of Social Medicine and Community Health, Jawaharlal Nehru University, New Delhi- 110078
9. **Dr Aditya Kumar Patra**, Lecturer in Economics, Kalinga Mahavidyalaya, G.Udayagiri, Kandhamal, Orissa, 762100
10. **Arabinda Acharya**, Research Scholar, GIPE, Pune, Maharashtra
11. **R.L.Panigrahy**
12. **Dr. Bandana Gaur,** Associate, Professor Deptt. of Sociology & Pol. Sc., DEI, DayalBagh, Agra.

CHAPTER

Alcohol, Sexual Violence and HIV/AIDS in Karnataka

Exploring the Possible Relationship

—Sateesh Gouda M. and Dr. A.G. Khan

Introduction

Though India is traditionally perceived to be a 'dry' culture, but alcohol use in some form has always existed in the country. The view of alcohol as impure and polluting, that many middle class Indians have been predominantly influenced by Western temperance campaigners in the 19th century. A view which acquired greater popularity during the Nationalist movement and was shaped into a generally held belief that drinking alcohol was alien to Indian culture. However, the link between alcohol use and sexual behaviour has serious implications for the health of populations particularly due to the advent of HIV infection. The WHO coordinated a multi-country study to identify factors related to risky sexual behaviour among alcohol users in diverse cultural settings. The countries involved Belarus, India, Mexico, Kenya, Romania, the Russian Federation, South Africa and Zambia. The results of the study presented in a form of report are likely to be useful to respond in specific and appropriate ways to the problem of alcohol use and sexual risk behaviour.

Sexual violence is a serious public health and criminal justice problem. Many men and women suffer sexual violence, a number of whom experience severe physical injuries or subsequently develop mental health problems. Alcohol is an important dimension in sexual violence many perpetrators are drinking when they attack their victims or have alcohol abuse problems. Sexual violence is defined as:

> "any sexual act, attempt to obtain a sexual act, unwanted sexual comments or advances, or acts to traffic, or otherwise directed, against a person's sexuality using coercion, by any person regardless of their relationship to the victim, in any setting, including but not limited to home and work."

The report shows that 1.5 per cent of women consume alcohol among them almost every day 0.3 per cent, about once a week 0.5 per cent and less often 0.6 per cent, if we see the frequency of alcohol consumption of men often 12.5 per cent and sometimes 20.4 per cent.

Why People Drink Alcohol?

Across project sites studied in the WHO report drinking was manifested as a lifestyle and indispensable part of social life, integral in partnership development and functional in sexual encounters. In all the countries except in India alcohol consumption was believed to signify maleness. In South Africa, for example, "being able to hold one's drink and drink heavily were regarded as sign of masculinity". The report concludes that being under the influence of alcohol was culturally accepted as an excuse for irresponsible behaviour, including risky sex, in Kenya and South Africa, in Mexico, as well as in Belarus, Romania and the Russian Federation. In Romania, alcohol consumption was not only culturally accepted as an excuse for irresponsible behaviour but also as an excuse that specifically applied to men, implying that alcohol use-related irresponsible behaviour was culturally accepted as an assertion/manifestation of maleness.

In Kenya it was observed that "alcohol use was believed to reduce fears connected to sex and encouraged risky sex, and to provide extra power for sex"; and in South Africa some research participants noted that "alcohol use and sex were a match made in heaven". In Mexico "young people and homosexual men used alcohol to build courage to approach a possible sexual contact". The research results also indicated that in India "alcohol's positive effect on arousal and pleasure was particularly reported by high-risk groups". In Belarus "alcohol use was perceived as very important in sexual activity", with some persons noting that alcohol use during sexual intercourse made "them become more attractive". It was also found in Belarus that alcohol use was the third most frequent reason for girls to have sex the first time. In Romania it was noted that, as a rule, "alcohol was taken as a socializer and a facilitator of sex". In the Russian Federation "there was a common misconception that a person without alcohol was incapable of engaging in sex".

The WHO reports points to the fact that certain groups are in particular vulnerable to the combination of alcohol and risky sex; female commercial sex workers (FCSW), truck drivers and youth:

> "Alcohol use and sexual risk behaviour go hand in hand in commercial sex encounters. FCSWs use alcohol to cope with the pressures of their work, e.g. a large number of sexual encounters. Many a times they and their clients use alcohol together. Condom use is more evident among paying sex partners than non-paying sex partners of sex workers. Brothel-based workers are able to negotiate condom use better than non-brothel-based workers in India. Most studies suggest that there is greater consistency of condom use in commercial sex than in private encounters, but that levels of alcohol use do not necessarily alter levels of condom use. However, clients' alcohol use has emerged as an important determinant of condom use in some studies. Other studies have found no differences in condom use between FCSWs who use alcohol and those who do not. Drinking alcohol and visiting commercial sex workers are evident among long-distance drivers all over the world. Transport workers

and migrant populations who frequently visit FCSWs, spread STIs and HIV infection from one place to the other and from high-risk groups to the general population. IDUs (injecting drug users) who are sexually active contribute to the spread of HIV infection in Belarus, the Russian Federation, Romania and India. Alcohol use, especially among young adolescents, is associated with casual sex encounters, traffic accidents, violence, crime and social problems (e.g. in Belarus, South Africa, Mexico). Early sexual experience, a high level of risk taking and alcohol use increase the risk of contracting STIs and HIV among adolescents."

Specific Findings on Alcohol use and Sexual Hehaviour in India

An earlier study found that women's alcoholism was relatively low and most other Indian studies have found very low rates of alcohol use in women in India (Murthy and Benegal 1995). As part of a community epidemiological study by NIMHANS, a community survey in the catchment area of NIMHANS, employing a face to face interview of 1956 subjects found the prevalence of alcohol dependence (ICD-9 303.0) to be 3.79 per cent (Study on Severe Mental Morbidity, ICMR). For our purposes we have assumed a conservative estimate of 30 percent prevalence of alcohol use and 3.79 percent alcohol dependence. The comparative figures in the USA are 70 percent and 7.41 percent respectively (Grant *et al.*, 1994).

The WHO reports (2002) that Alcohol use was common among men, but very rare among women, except for tribal/traditional folk artists and sex workers. The degree to which alcohol was accepted varied across socio-economic and cultural group and might be linked to an overall lifestyle that includes the consumption of non-vegetarian food and liberal sexual attitudes. The complementary occurrence of alcohol use and group sex or homosexuality should be seen as an indicator of strong cultural barriers to any sexual "otherness", which could only be broken under the facilitating effect of alcohol. All participants from risk groups were alcohol drinkers. The majority drank alcohol alone at home or at the workplace in the evening. Cannabis/other psychoactive substances was used by half the participating transport workers and by 15 percent of the FCSWs. Opiates were used by 3 percent of the general population sample but by 13 percent of the transport workers.

Alcohol at first intercourse: 20 per cent, Premarital sex: 20 per cent, Man-to-man sex (lifetime experience) among 8.5 per cent of general population, and 9 percent among transport workers, Non-regular non-commercial sex among general population: 18 percent, MSMs in general population frequently engaged in anal sex, always without condoms, Condom use during last intercourse with regular sex partners: 11-15 percent, Condom used during last intercourse with non-regular partners: about 66.6 percent, Condom use was low except among FCSWs (79 percent during last intercourse), although they reported low condom use during sex with non-paying clients, who were partners for whom intimacy was reserved. Condom use with commercial clients ensured FCSWs of a sort of psychological protection, Some people still believed in the traditional myth that HIV transmission could be prevented by cleaning the genitalia with alcohol, urine or antiseptic solutions, finishing the sexual act quickly, or ejaculating “outside”.

HIV/AIDS and India

India has a population of one billion, around half of whom are adults in the sexually active age group. The first AIDS case in India was detected in 1986; since then HIV infection has been reported in all States and union territories. The spread of HIV in India has been diverse, with much of India having a low rate of infection and the epidemic being most extreme in the southern half of the country and in the far north-east. The highest HIV prevalence rates are found in Maharashtra, Andhra Pradesh and Karnataka in the south;

and Manipur, Mizoram and Nagaland in the north-east. Four southern States (Andhra Pradesh, Maharashtra, Tamil Nadu and Karnataka) account for around 63 percent of all people living with HIV in India. In the southern States, HIV is primarily spread through heterosexual contact, whereas infections are mainly found amongst injecting drug users and sex workers in the north-east.

The National Family Health Survey conducted between 2005 and 2006 measured HIV prevalence among the general adult population of India. The survey found the rate among men to be considerably higher than that among women. i.e. HIV prevalence total age 15-49 among men 0.36 percent and 0.22 percent among women counts to total 0.28 percent. The average HIV prevalence among women attending antenatal clinics in India is 0.60 percent. Much higher rates are found among people attending sexually transmitted disease clinics (3.74 percent), female sex workers (4.90 percent), injecting drug users (6.92 percent) and men who have sex with men (6.41 percent). (Sources: NFHS-3 and NACO-2007)

HIV/AIDS and Karnataka

Karnataka is one of four large southern India States with a relatively advanced HIV epidemic, with the adult HIV prevalence in several districts exceeding one per cent for the past 9 years. As a part of the National AIDS Control Programme (NACP) of the National AIDS Control Organization (NACO), Karnataka has been conducting the HIV Sentinel Surveillance since 1998. Surveillance is carried out annually by testing for HIV at designated sentinel sites. Testing for infection is conducted among populations at higher risk, represented by patients at sexually transmitted disease (STD) clinics, intravenous drug users (IDUs) who often share needles, female sex workers (FSWs), and men who have sex with men (MSM). Populations at low risk are represented by women attending antenatal clinics (ANCs).

Pregnant women attending antenatal clinics are assumed to have the same risk of sexual transmission of HIV as any other sexually active general population. The prevalence among ANC attendees in 2006 is 1.13 percent while NFHS-3 provides estimate of 0.69percent in 2006.

Review of Literature: Explaining the Seriousness of Alcohol

***Sudha Sivaram** (2006):* In India, more men than women consume alcohol, and alcohol can be easily obtained from wine shops, bars, discotheques and pubs. These locations are often spread out in a given geographical area, and as such are not specific to any socio-economic class. Alcoholic beverages are available in three categories: Indian-made foreign liquor (IMFL), country liquor and illicit liquor [WHO 2002]. The IMFL has a maximum alcohol content of 42.8 percent and includes whisky, rum and brandy. Country liquor has an alcohol content of about 40 per cent and is a distilled beverage made from grain and crops such as rice, palm and sugarcane. Popular among poorer populations are illicit, home-brewed liquors where the alcohol content varies up to 56 per cent. According to the World Health Organization, such brews account for more than half the alcohol consumed in terms of quantity. With recent economic liberalization policies, alcohol has become more available, with more varieties and outlets [Basu K 1998]. This ease of access is reflected in surveys that assess alcohol sales and prevalence in India. 6 per cent to 75 per cent of those surveyed in Indian states report using alco-hol, and studies investigating dependence report reliably that approximately 50 per cent of those who drink alcohol are dependent on it [Benegal, 2005] Calling for more attention to social and health impacts of alcohol use, qualita-tive studies report that heavy drinking re-sults in a high burden of domestic discord and violence in India [Chowdhury, *et al.*, 2006] However, the relationship between al-cohol and HIV risk is only beginning to be explored in India. International studies suggest that alcohol use may increase risk for unsafe sex [Dermen, 1998] by impairing cognitive reasoning and condom use during sex [Steele and Josephs 1990] and by aggravating individual differences in particular sexual situations

One of the most striking indicators of the growing alcohol related problems in the country is the proportion of patients being admitted to various psychiatric treatment centers in different parts of the country (Isaac, 1998). At centre in NIMHANS, for example registrations for alcohol related neuropsychiatric problems (including alcohol dependence) increased from 212 in 1985 to 995 in 1994, and presently constitutes more than 10 percent of all registrations in the Psychiatry department. This rise appears closely correlated with rise in sales of alcohol in the state (Pearsons corr. coeff $p<0.05$).

Effect of Alcohol Consumption

Benegal *et al.*, (2000). NIMHANS Projecting the data obtained at the micro level, the estimations show that the social cost of alcoholism in the State of Karnataka given that there are 5 lakh alcohol dependent individuals as deduced from the 3.79 per cent prevalence of alcohol dependence syndrome in the State. External costs include health care provided by the health care system of the State for detoxification and counseling. The cost per person per day in NIMHANS has been calculated at Rs. 600 (including establishment costs, salaries and consumables) by the NIMHANS administration. With a mean of 38.42 days per admission and a mean of 2.06 admissions over 2 years, the cost of health care in a year assuming all alcohol dependent individuals in the State undergo at least one admission in a year is Rs. 1129.39 crores (this figure has been adjusted for those who pay for their own treatment). Costs of alcohol related medical and surgical problems (data are available for head injury only) amount to Rs. 0.15 crores. Other high risk behaviour is also prominently associated with alcohol misuse. While HIV positive alcoholics are increasingly encountered, the numbers are yet small and undocumented.

Alcohol and Sexual Violence

The WHO (2005) report: "Alcohol Use and Sexual Risk Behaviour: A Cross-Cultural Study in Eight Countries" points out some key patterns of interaction between alcohol use and sexual behaviour, based on review of available research literature and empirical studies in eight countries; Kenya, South Africa, Zambia, Mexico, Belarus, Romania, The Russian Federation and India. Analysis of the data in the WHO report showed that not only did alcohol use and sexual behaviour separately pose risks for STI/HIV infection, but also collectively. In a number of ways alcohol use and sexual behaviour and beliefs actively "supported" one another, with alcohol use and beliefs acting as both precursors and outcomes of sexual behaviour. The particular manner in which alcohol use and sexual behaviour interacted, however, varied to some extent across the eight countries.

Sexual assault of adolescent and adult women has been called a silent epidemic, because it occurs at high rates yet is rarely reported to the authorities (Koss 1988). Several reasons contribute to the under-reporting of sexual assault cases. Many victims do not tell others about the assault, because they fear that they will not be believed or will be derogated, which, according to research findings, is a valid concern (Abbey et al. 1996b). Other victims may not realize that they have actually experienced legally defined rape or sexual assault, because the incident does not fit the prototypic scenario of "stranger rape". For example, in a study by Abbey and colleagues (1996b), a woman wrote, "For years I believed it was my fault for being too drunk. I never called it 'rape' until much more recently, even though repeatedly told him 'no'.

Raul Caetano (2001) Intimate partner violence (IPV) is a major public health problem in the United States. Results from a 1995 national study indicated that 23 percent of the black couples, 11.5 percent of the white couples, and 17 percent of the Hispanic couples surveyed reported an incident of male-to-female partner violence in the 12 months preceding the survey. The rate of female-to-male partner violence was also high: 15 percent among white couples, 30 percent among black couples, and 21 percent among Hispanic couples. The higher prevalence of IPV among ethnic minorities, compared with whites, cannot be explained by any single factor, but seems to be related to risk factors associated with the individual, the type of relationship between partners, and factors in the environment. Alcohol plays an important part in IPV. The study found that 30 to 40 percent of the men and 27 to 34 percent of the women who perpetrated violence against their partners were drinking at the time of the event. Alcohol-related problems were associated with IPV among blacks and whites, but not among Hispanics.

Several studies have shown that socio-economic status is an important variable to consider when exploring the association between alcohol use and IPV. Straus and Smith (1990) found that the combined effects of urbanicity of residence, income, and younger age largely explained differences in severe violence between Hispanics and whites. Reanalyzing these same data, Kantor and colleagues (1993) also found that differences in severe husband-to-wife violence among Hispanics and whites were attributable to socioeconomic factors and drinking. These data support the social-structural theory but not the subculture of violence theory. However, differences in severe husband-to-wife violence between blacks and whites cannot be attributed to the effects of socioeconomic factors (Cazenave and Straus 1990) or to the combined effects of socioeconomic factors and alcohol use (Kantor *et al.,* 1993). In other words, when differences in socioeconomic status and alcohol use between blacks and whites are kept constant, blacks' higher rate of IPV does not disappear.

The British Crime Survey estimates that one in ten women has been sexually victimised since age 16 (Myhill and Allen, 2002). Many perpetrators have drunk alcohol immediately prior to the incident and/or have drinking problems (Grubin and Gunn, 1990). Perpetrator alcohol consumption is sometimes associated with increased sexual violation and physical aggression (Brecklin and Ullman, 2002). The tendency for drinking to be a shared activity, the pharmacological effects of alcohol and beliefs and expectations about the effects of alcohol are important in explaining why sexual violence is frequently committed by or against people who have been drinking.

IIPS (2006): Violence against women is a serious problem in India. Overall, one-third of women age 15-49 have experienced physical violence and about 1 in 10 have experienced sexual violence. In total, 35 percent have experienced physical or sexual violence. This figure translates into millions of women who have suffered, and continue to suffer, at the hands of husbands and other family members. NFHS-3 findings underscore the extent and severity of violence against women in India, especially married women. Women married to men who get drunk frequently are more than twice as likely to experience violence as women whose husbands do not drink alcohol at all.

Singh, KK (2004): A survey of 3,412 married men aged 15-59 was conducted in undivided Uttar Pradesh. Analysis takes into account the pre-marital, and extra marital sexual activity of men and alcohol user. Logistic model is applied to observe the influence of alcohol use on risk behaviour of married men after controlling socio-demographic variables. Alcohol use has been found to be a very strong determinant which effects the risk behaviour of married men i.e. extra-marital sex in undivided Uttar Pradesh controlling other socio-demographic variables. Thus, programs may be launched targeting to the men who are mainly using alcohol.

Alcohol and Risk of HIV

Privileges attached to drunken behaviour: People who drink to excess, either on single occasions or regularly, are more likely than others to engage in behaviour that place them at risk for contracting HIV. They will more often be present at locations where the risk is higher and more often engage in sexual risk-taking, like having multiple partners, casual partners or unprotected sex. Under the influence of alcohol people loose their inhibitions and have their judgment impaired and can easily find themselves involved in behaviour that would put them at risk for contracting HIV. Such behaviour can not alone be attributed to the physical effects of alcohol on the brain and the body, maybe not at all! The explanation is more likely to be of a cultural, social and psychological kind. In many societies and cultures, in all corners of the world, irresponsible or rude behaviour under alcohol intoxication is tolerated and even pardoned. With this cultural acceptance in mind, people use alcohol as an excuse to perform actions that are normally not tolerated or as an explanation of failure, like poor sexual performance. In other words, drinking gives you privileges and these privileges are accepted by others.

Reason for Concern

Abbey, *et al.,* (2001): Conservative estimates of sexual assault prevalence suggest that 25 per cent of American women have experienced sexual assault, including rape. Approximately one-half of those cases involve alcohol consumption by the perpetrator, victim, or both. Alcohol contributes to sexual assault through multiple pathways, often exacerbating existing risk factors. Beliefs about alcohol's effects on sexual and aggressive behavior, stereotypes about drinking women, and alcohol's effects on cognitive and motor skills contribute to alcohol-involved sexual assault. Despite advances in researchers' understanding of the relationships between alcohol consumption and sexual assault, many questions still need to be addressed in future studies.

There is generally an increase in alcohol use by teenagers and women. Men, however, generally have more social liberties than women, with respect to alcohol use as well as sexual activities. Furthermore, the literature shows that the age for initiating alcohol use and experimenting with sex is on the decline, but the age for marriage is on the rise (e.g. the Russian Federation, India). Teenage pregnancies are also on the rise. Sexual experimentation outside marriage is increasing. Risky sexual behaviours continue despite a confirmed STI/HIV status, as reported in Belarus, Zambia and India. Denial of the problem and social stigma prevent people with STIs to seek treatment. Severity of symptoms is another factor that influences the decision of persons with STIs to seek treatment. Despite knowledge about preventive measures, condom use is limited. The spread of the HIV epidemic from high-risk groups to the general population is a concern in a populous country like India. Male dominance also limits the ability of women to adopt preventive measures such as the use of condoms.

Raynard (2005): Research findings clearly show that the use of alcohol and other substances of abuse is a factor in the spread of HIV and can complicate the long-term health outcomes of HIV-positive individuals. Therefore it is important that health care providers screen their HIV patients for alcohol use problems and those patients being treated for alcohol and other substance use be screened for HIV infection. In both cases, steps should be taken to ensure that HIV-positive patients have access to appropriate care.

Groups Vulnerable to Alcohol use, Risky Sexual Behaviour and HIV in India

The National Behavioural Sentinel Surveys among high-risk groups in India showed that alcohol use (at least once a week) is increasing among female commercial sex workers (FCSWs), their clients, among men having sex with men (MSMs), and among injecting drug users (IDUs). A number of these groups reported regular alcohol use before sex (FCSWs 15 per cent; clients of FCSWs 13 per cent; MSMs 36 per cent). High rates of alcohol use have also been observed among vulnerable groups such as adolescents, commercial sex workers and their clients in other countries (e.g. South Africa, Belarus, Romania and Mexico).

Stoner *et al.*, 2006: It is plausible and recognized that alcohol use impacts unsafe sexual activity, the precise mechanisms of this association are still being researched. In our work in southern India, we conducted open-ended interviews with patrons of community-based alcohol outlets or wine shops in Chennai city in southern India. Analysis of these interviews suggests four factors that might influence this mechanism. First is the role of disinhibition and increased bravado in encouraging risky sexual behaviour that wine shop patrons attribute to alcohol consumption. Second is the role of the individual's social background in driving both alcohol dependence and risky sex following alcohol use. A third factor is the absence of sexual communica-tion between men and their regular partners. The fourth factor is the role of personal and social networks.

Contradictory to all the above mentioned studies few studies found that there is no relation alcohol and risky sexual behaviour. The association between drinking levels and high-risk sexual behavior does not imply that alcohol necessarily plays a direct role in such behavior or that it causes high-risk behavior on every occasion (Dermen, K.H, 2000). For example, bars and drinking parties serve as convenient social settings for meeting potential sexual partners. In addition, alcohol abuse occurs frequently among people whose lifestyle or personality predisposes them to high-risk behaviors in general (Stall, R *et al.*, 2001).

Need for the Study

In recent time there are many studies at global level prove the seriousness of alcohol consumption on sexual life and risk of HIV/AIDS. It is known that there are very few studies available in India to support the seriousness of alcohol consumption on risk of HIV/AIDS; even studies are very less at Karnataka level. Here NFHS-3 provides an opportunity to analysis the data and to prove the risk of HIV and sexual violence with appropriate evidence.

Objective

Based on the above conceptual built up, an was made in this article to study the role of alcohol in contribution sexual risk in different settings and populations across the state. However, in order to meet the above objective the NFHS -3 Karnataka data was used for the analysis purpose. Moreover the important forms of violence to be considered are physical, sexual and emotional one, are tried to test and analyzed in the forth coming paragraph.

Data Source

Data for this study has been obtained from the National Family Health Survey (NFHS-3), conducted in 2005-06. national sample survey designed to provide information on population, family planning, maternal and child health, child survival, AIDS and sexually transmitted infections (STIs), nutrition of children, women and men and women's status in Karnataka. NFHS-3 collected information from a nationally representative sample of 5342 households, 6008 women age 15-49, and 5528 men age 15-54, from among all the women and men interviewed in Karnataka. NFHS-3 provides estimates of HIV prevalence for adult women and men at the state level, 10119 (5366 women and 4754 men) were tested for HIV. The available data on women aged 15-49 years were analyzed to find out the whether partner or Husband consume alcohol. NFHS-3 collected information from married and unmarried women age 15-49 about their experience of physical and sexual violence. Married women were also asked about their experience of emotional violence.

Methodology

Bivariate analysis has been carried out to see differential in husband's alcohol consumption by selected socio-economic and demographic variables and to see the risk of HIV and STD on women because of husband's alcohol conception. Further, in order to isolate the effects of independent variables on dependent variable, multivariate analysis resorting to logistic regression is carried out. In logistic regression to see the controlled effect of alcohol consumption on HIV risk and STD, we have taken the socio-economic and demographic variables as controlling variables. All the analysis done in this paper is for those currently married women who are selected for household relation section interview.

Profile of Karnataka

Karnataka is bordered by the Arabian Sea to the west, Goa to the northwest, Maharashtra to the north, Andhra Pradesh to the east, Tamil Nadu to the southeast, and Kerala to the southwest. The state covers an area of 74,122 sq miles (191,976 km^2), or 5.83 per cent of the total geographical area of India. It is the eighth largest Indian State by area, the ninth largest by population and comprises 29 districts. Kannada is the official and most widely spoken language.

Demographic: According to the 2001 census of India, the total population of Karnataka is 52,850,562, of which 26,898,918 (50.89 per cent) are male and 25,951,644 (49.11 per cent) are female, or 1000 males for every 964 females. This represents a 17.25 percent increase over the population in 1991. The population density is 275.6 per km^2 and 33.98 percent of the people live in urban areas.

Social: The literacy rate is 66.6 percent with 76.1 percent of males and 56.9 percent of females being literate. 83 percent of the population are Hindu, 11 percent are Muslim, 4 percent are Christian, 0.78 percent are Jains, 0.73 percent are Buddhist, and with the remainder belonging to other religions.

Economic: Karnataka, which had an estimated GSDP (Gross State Domestic Product) of about Rs. 2152.82 billion ($ 51.25 billion) in the 2007-2008 fiscal year, is one of the more economically progressive states in India. Karnataka had an estimated poverty ratio of 17 percent, less than the national ratio of 27.5 percent.(The Planning Commission GO 2006-07I). Nearly 56 percent of the workforce in Karnataka is engaged in agriculture and related activities. A total of 12.31 million hectares of land, or 64.6 percent of the state's total area, is cultivated. Much of the agricultural output is dependent on the southwest monsoon as only 26.5 percent of the sown area is irrigated. (Department of Agriculture, GoK, 2006-07)

Health: In the field of super-specialty health care, Karnataka's private sector competes with the best in the world. Karnataka has also established a modicum of public health services having a better record of health care and child care than most other states of India. In spite of these advances, some parts of the state still leave much to be desired when it comes to primary health care, particularly Northern part and some policies in costal Karnataka region.

Table 1.1 : Percentage of Women who Reported Her Husband/ Partner Drinks Alcohol by Demographic and Economic Characteristics, Karnataka, NFHS-3, 2005-06

Demographic characteristics	Partner drinks alcohol	No. of women
	1	2
Respondent's age* **		
15 to 24 years	23.9	777
25 to 34 years	32.9	1466
35 and above	36.8	1201
Age at first marriage* **		
Below 18 years	36.0	1895

...*(Contd.)*

	1	2
18 to 25 years	28.2	1384
26 and above	22.6	164
No. of living children* **		
No children	21.9	352
1 child	29.9	642
2 children	30.9	1257
3 and more children	37.9	1192
Age difference between partners		
Respondent is older than partner	43.8	48
Both are same aged	24.1	58
partner is older for 1 to 5 years	30.2	1099
partner is older for 6 and above years	30.3	1989
Economic characteristics		
Standard of living* **		
Low	44.2	880
Medium	35.8	1097
High	22.1	1278
Respondent Working* **		
No	26.2	1968
Yes	40.4	1471
Partner's Occupation* **		
Managerial	26.5	407
Clerical or sales	19.4	501
Agricultural or Manual workers	35.5	2478
Respondent Occupation* **		
Not working/House wife	24.7	1751
Managerial	41.8	220
Clerical or sales	35.5	110
Agricultural or Manual workers	40.1	1363
Total	**32.2**	**3444**

***Indicates the value of Pearson Chi-square test is 0.01

Table 1.1 discusses the percentage of women who reported her husband drinks alcohol by women demographic and economic characteristics. Age is an important variable in any demographic studies, the table showing that as the age of the respondent increase the probability of husband drinking alcohol is increasing, it shows that as the age or the marital duration increases the control over husband is decreasing and husband going for alcohol become common. Age at marriage of women is also very important factor to see the relationship of the husband alcohol consumption because women at younger age have the less skills to convince her husband then the older women so marriage at older (after 21) is not only important for maternal health it helps develop good understanding between couples. The table supports the argument that, there is inverse relationship between age at marriage and husband drinking alcohol. As the Caldwell explains in his "*The intergenerational wealth flow theory of fertility decline*" the number of living children is also one of the important predictor in husband alcohol consumption. The table shows that there is positive relationship between alcohol consumption and number of living children. The possible reason may be children are used as source of income or due to the more children husband may feel more burdens and to avoid the tension husband may go for alcohol consumption.

So far we discussed the relationship of alcohol consumption with demographic variables. Now we can see the relationship of economic variables and alcohol consumption of husband. Standard of living is also very important factor to decide the economical status of person or the family through indirect way, there is common believe that as the people income increases they spend the money for enjoyment especially in alcohol, but the study show that there is inverse relationship between standard of living and alcohol consumption, possible reason may be people in the low standard are manual and agriculture workers. Here the effort was made to see the respondent's working status and husband alcohol consumption, the results are showing that the husband of working women go for more alcohol consumption. It can be explained in two ways, one reason may be husband drink alcohol because he has sufficient money to spend or other way respondent has compiled to go work because her husband drink alcohol because she has the responsibility to run the family. If we see the occupation of women and husband's and alcohol consumption, it shows that the husbands of respondent who works in Agricultural or manual workers drinks alcohol more (36 percent) compare to managerial and clerical work. So it is clear from the table that people who are going for alcohol are from unorganized sector, the possible reason may be because of hard labor work or people working in unorganized sector are mostly illiterate. If we see the relationship with respondent's occupation and her husband alcohol consumption, it shows that the husband's of the respondent who are in managerial position go for more alcohol consumption (42 percent) followed by husband's of respondent who work in the agricultural or manual workers (40 percent) compare to respondent those not working/housewife and clerical/sales.

Table 1.2 show the percentage of women who reported her husband drinks alcohol by women's social characteristics. Social variable also very important factor in determining the alcohol consumption of person, as we know people belong to lower caste and tribes go for more alcohol consumption even it is true from the ancient days, the study support that argument. People belonging to scheduled caste go for more (51 percent) alcohol followed by the scheduled tribes (41 percent) compared to other backward class and none of the any group (28 percent). It shows that still there is need for govt. intervention to make the people aware of adverse effect of alcohol consumption and the Pearson Chi-Square test also show that it is significant at one per cent level. The custom followed guided by the religion also play an important role in determining the alcohol consumption, the table showing that people belonging to Muslim go for less (20 percent) alcohol compare to Hindu (34 percent) and Other religion

Table 1.2 : Percentage of women who reported her Husband/ Partner drinks alcohol by social characteristics, Karnataka, NFHS-3, 2005-06.

	Partner drinks alcohol	No. of women
Type of caste* **		
Scheduled caste	51.3	534
Scheduled tribe	41.2	233
Other backward class	27.6	1906
None of them	27.9	766
Religion* **		
Hindu	33.5	2969
Muslim	20.2	347
Other Religion	34.6	127
Place of residence		
Urban	31.7	1370
Rural	32.6	2074
Exposure to mass media* **		
No	38.0	677
Partial	33.6	2148
Full	21.3	619
Education of the respondent* **		
No education	41.0	1405
Primary	34.4	471
Secondary	24.5	1336
Higher	19.5	231
Education of the Partner/Husband* **		
No education	40.4	1068
Primary	39.4	475
Secondary	27.9	1469
Higher	18.8	425
Total	**32.2**	**3444**

*** indicates the value of Pearson Chi-Square test is <0.01.

(35 percent) and the Pearson Chi-Square test also shows it is significant at 1 percent level. The effort was done to see the is there any difference of alcohol consumption behaviour by the place of residence, however it shows that there is no much difference in the behaviour of alcohol consumption on the basis of place of residence. The government has been making lot of effort reach/convince the people from different type of Medias. The table showing that there is an positive effect of exposure of mass media, people those have full exposure to mass media go less for (21 percent) alcohol compare to the people no exposure (38 percent) and partial exposure (34 percent). It shows that there should be some more effort to reach the people through media. Education is one of the important variable which make difference in many demographic and economic factors i.e. number of living children, age at marriage etc. here also the effort was done to see the how far the education influence alcohol consumption by respondent's education and her husband education. The table shows that there is inverse relationship between education and alcohol consumption in both respondents as well her husband education.

Table 1.3 : Effect of partner's alcohol consumption on women health Karnataka, NFHS-3, 2005-06

	Partner drinks alcohol		
	No	Yes	Total
	1	2	3
Result of HIV test*			
Negative	99.5	98.9	99.3
Positive	0.5	1.1	0.7
Number of women	2062	1002	3064
Had genital discharge in last 12 month			
No	97.8	97.6	97.7
Yes	2.2	2.4	2.3

	1	2	3
Number of women	2323	1107	3430
Experienced any sexual violence ***			
No	98.2	91.6	96.0
Yes	1.8	8.4	4.0
Number of women	2332	1111	3443
Respondent Drinks alcohol***			
No	99.6	96.1	98.5
Yes	0.4	3.9	1.5
Number of women	2332	1110	3442
Husband has other wives***			
No	97.6	95.2	96.9
Yes	2.4	4.8	3.1
Number of women	2223	966	3189
Husband has other wives			
Had genital discharge in last 12 months**			
No	97.8	92.9	97.6
Yes	2.2	7.1	2.4
Number of women	3078	99	3177

* indicates the value of Pearson Chi-Square test is <0.1.

** indicates the value of Pearson Chi-Square test is <0.05.

***indicates the value of Pearson Chi-Square test is <0.01

Effect of alcohol consumption on women health and sexual life

Table 1.3 discusses the effect of husband's alcohol consumption on women different aspects of health. In recent past the link between alcohol use and HIV risk exposure and treatment has been observed in many locations around the world. Very recently drinking has been in relation to the sexuality and violence came into the picture in India. The WHO reports points to the fact that certain groups are in particular vulnerable to the combination of alcohol and risky sex; female commercial sex workers (FCSW), truck drivers and youth: "Alcohol use and sexual risk behaviour go hand in hand in commercial sex encounters. FCSWs use alcohol to cope with the pressures of their work. In this regard the effort was made to see the relationship between husband's alcohol consumption and respondent risk of HIV/AIDS infection. The analysis proved that alcohol consumption of partner or husband has the high risk (1.1 percent) of getting HIV/AIDS compare to the respondent (0.5 percent) those husbands don't drink alcohol and Pearson Chi-square test shows that it is significant at 10 percent level. Sexually Transmitted Disease (STD) is also one of the important factor to understand the sexual risk of women, here an effort was done to see the that whether women those husband drinks alcohol has any risk of STD. So we have selected the variable whether respondent had genital discharge in last 12 months by which indirectly we can understand the risk of STD. The study shows that women those husband drink alcohol had reported more (2.4 percent) genital discharge in last 12 months compare to those respondent's (2.2%) husband don't drink alcohol, however it is not significant statistically.

Sexual violence is a serious public health and criminal justice problem. Many men and women suffer sexual violence, a number of who experience severe physical injuries or subsequently develop mental health problems. Alcohol is an important dimension in sexual violence many perpetrators are drinking when they attack their victims or have alcohol abuse problems

Violence is an common act which often women experience after her husband drinking alcohol. Table shows that women those husband drink alcohol has reported more (8.4 percent) sexual violence compared to those women (1.8 percent)

husband doesn't drink alcohol and it is significant at 1 percent level. Chowdhury and collogues paid more attention to social and health impacts of alcohol use, qualita-tive studies report that heavy drinking re-sults in a high burden of domestic discord and violence in India.

Women alcohol consumption also have the adverse affect on her health as well as it will leads to sexual risk. Here an attempt was done to see who goes for alcohol consumption among women. Table 1.3 shows that women those husband drink alcohol go more (3.9%) for alcohol consumption than those women's (0.4%) husband doesn't drink alcohol. It shows that men behavior has very important impact on his wife behaviour. Person having more than one wife also have very important implication for risk of sexual life. So researcher interested to see whether alcohol contribute to have more than one wife, the study proves that those women's husband drink alcohol are more (4.8%) chance to have more than one wife compare to women (2.4%) those husband don't drink alcohol. It shows that alcohol consumption have positive impact to have more than one wife. As we discussed earlier, having more than one wife has risk of sexual behaviour, the table shows that women reported more (5.8%) genital discharge in last 12 months compare to women (2.1) whose husband don't have more than one wife and it is significant at 5 percent level. Further table shows that how husband having more than one wife have the impact on sexual health, it shows that women are exposed for more (7.1%) risk for genital discharge compare to women those husband not having wife other than the respondent.

Table 1.4 discuss the Logistic regression for different variables influenced by alcohol consumption. In order to isolate the effects of independent variables on dependent variable, multivariate analysis resorting to logistic regression is carried out. To get the effect of husband's alcohol consumption on each variable the logistic regression has been

Table 1.4 : Logistic Regression for Different Variables Influenced by Alcohol Consumption NFHS-3, Karnataka

Indicators		Exp(B) (2005-06)	
		Un-controlled	Controlled
Drink alcohol	**Result of HIV test[1]**		
	No®		
	Yes	2.09*	1.60
Drink alcohol	**Had genital discharge in last 12 month[2]**		
	No®		
	Yes	1.08	1.02
Drink alcohol	**Experienced any sexual violence[3]**		
	No®		
	Yes	4.80***	3.54***
Drink alcohol	**Respondent drink alcohol[4]**		
	No®		
	Yes	9.71***	6.99***
Drink alcohol	**Husband has other wives[5]**		
	No®		
	Yes	2.09***	1.89***
Husband has other wives	**Had genital discharge in last 12 months[6]**		
	No®		
	Yes	9.71***	2.50**

* indicates significant at 10 percent level.

** indicates significant at 5 percent level.

***indicates significant at 1 percent level.

® indicates reference category.

1. Dependent variable: Result of HIV test 0=Negative, 1 = Positive
2. Dependent variable: Had genital discharge in last 12 month 0 = N0, 1 = Yes
3. Dependent variable: Experienced any sexual violence 0 = N0, 1 = Yes
4. Dependent variable: Respondent drink alcohol 0 = N0, 1 = Yes
5. Dependent variable: Husband has other wives0 = N0, 1 = Yes
6. Dependent variable: had genital discharge in last 12 month 0 = N0, 1 = Yes

Note: to get the controlled value logistic regression for all the variables, demographic, economic and social variables have been used except the genital discharge in last 12 months.

used. Multivariate analysis is the simultaneous analysis of three or more variables. It is frequently used to see whether a relationship between two variables remains when a third variable, called the control variable, is taken into account. Multivariate analyses are also done to determine the separate and joint effects of two variables upon a dependent variable. In this table dependent variables are result of HIV test (0=Negative, 1=Positive), Had genital discharge in last 12 month (0=No, 1=Yes), Experienced any sexual violence (0=No, 1=Yes), Respondent drink alcohol (0=No, 1=Yes), Husband has other wives (0=No, 1=Yes) and husband drink alcohol (No=0 and Yes=1) to see the risk of husband having more than one wife we have taken whether women had genital discharge in last 12 month (0=No, 1=Yes) as dependent variable and husband had other wife (No=0 and Yes=1) independent variable. To see whether a relationship between two variables remains when a socio-economic and social variable, called the control variable, is taken into account. Controlled comparisons are used to test the association between husband alcohol consumption on women health variables within specified levels of a third variable. The third variables are demographic, social and economic variables.

Table 1.4 explain the controlled and uncontrolled effect of alcohol consumption on different variables for controlling the variable we have taken the socio-economic and demographic variables such as age, marital duration, religion, caste, education, place of residence exposure to mass media, occupation, age difference between couples, no of living children etc. However to see the effect of husband having other wife we have taken only women individual variables as controlling variables. For uncontrolled value only husband drinks alcohol is independent variable and other variables like result of HIV/AIDS test, Had any genital discharge in last 12 months, experience any sexual violence, respondent drinks alcohol are dependent variables.

The table shows that the women those husband drink alcohol are 2.09 times more likely to get HIV/AIDS and in controlled value women those husband drink alcohol are 1.6 times more likely to get HIV/AIDS compare to those women whose husband don't drink alcohol. Since the other socio economic variables also play an important role determining the women health we have taken only controlled value for our discussion. Those reported her husband drink alcohols are 1.02 more likely to experience the genital discharge compare to women whose husband don't drink alcohol. If we see the women sexual violence after consumption those women reported her husband drink alcohol are 3.5 times more likely to experience sexual violence compare to non drinkers wife and it is significant at one percent level. Alcohol consumption motivate person to have more than one wife, those women who reported her husband drink alcohol are 7 times more likely to have more than wife compare to non drinking husband. At the same it is statistically proved that having more than one wife has sexual risk. The table shows that those women have more than one wife are 2.5 more likely to experience genital discharge.

REFERENCES

Abbey, A, Zawacki, T. Buck, P.O., Clinton, A. and McAuslan, P. (2001) "Alcohol and Sexual Assault", *Alcohol Health and Research World*, 25 (1), 43–51.

Abbey, A.; Ross, L.T.; Mcduffie, D.; and Mcauslan, P. (1996b) "Alcohol, misperception, and sexual assault: How and why are they linked?" *Evolutionary and Feminist Perspectives,* pp. 138-161.

Basu, K. (1998)"Globalization and Culture," *India Today* 20 April.

Benegal V Velayudhan A, Jain S, (2000) Social Costs of Alcoholism: A Karnataka Perspective. *NIMHANS Journal*,

Benegal, V., "India: alcohol and public health," Addiction 100, no. 8 (2005):1051-6.

C.M.Steele and R.A. Josephs, (1990) "Alcohol Myopia: Its prized and dangerous effects," *American Psychologist,* 45, no.8: 921-933.

Cazenave, N.A, and Straus, MA, (1990) "Race, class network embeddedness, and family violence: A search for potent support systems. In: Straus, Physical Violence in American Families: Risk Factors and Adaptations to Violence in 8,145 Families". *New Brunswick*, NJ: Transaction Books,. pp. 321-335.

Chowdhury, A.N., Ramakrishna J, Chakraborty A.K, and Weiss M.G, (2006) "Cultural context and impact of alco-hol use in the Sundarban Delta, West Bengal, India," *Social Science and Medicine* 63, no. 3 722-31.

Dermen, K.H, and Cooper, M.L. "Inhibition conflict and alcohol expectancy as moderators of alcohol's relationship to condom use", "Experimental and Clinical Psychopharmacology" 8(2):198–206, 2000.

Dermen, KH, Cooper ML, Agocha VB. (1998) "Sex-related alcohol expectancies as moderators of the relationship between alcohol use and risky sex in adolescents". *Journal of Studies on Alcohol*; 59: 71–77.

Grubin and Gunn (1990), "The imprisoned rapist and rape", *Journal of Addiction*, 80, 351-355

IIPS and Macro International (2007) *National Family Health survey report vol-1 (NFHS-3), 2005 -2006*, International Institute for Population Sciences, Mumbai.

Isaac M (1998) "Contemporary Trends: India". In Alcohol and Emerging Markets, Patterns,

Kantor, G.K.; Jasinski, J.; and Aldarondo, E. (1993) "Incidence of Hispanic Drinking and Intra-Family Violence", Paper presented at the annual meeting of the Research Society on Alcoholism in San Antonio, Texas.

Koss, M.P., and Dinero, T.E. (1988) "Predictors of sexual aggression among a national sample of male college students", *Annals of the New York Academy of Sciences,* 528:133-147,

Moeller, FG, Dougherty DM. Antisocial personality disorder, alcohol and aggression. Alcohol Research and Health, 2001, 25:5–11.WHO, 2005 Alcohol Use And Sexual Risk Behaviour: A Cross-Cultural Study In Eight Countries - WHO, Geneva

Murthy, P.J.N.V. & Benegal, V.(1995) Alcoholism in women. Paper presented at 47th ANCIPS Patna.

Myhill, A. and Allen, J. (2002). Rape and sexual assault of women: the extent and nature of the problem. Findings from the British Crime Survey. Home Office Research Study 237. London: Home Office.

Myhill, A. and Allen, J. (2002). Rape and sexual assault of women: the extent and nature of the problem. Findings from the British Crime Survey. Home Office Research Study 237. London: Home Office.on alcohol and drug abuse, (ed) Ray, R. & Pickens, R.W. NIMHANS Publication No. 20, Bangalore.

Raul, Caetano, John Schafer, Carol B. Cunradi (2001) Alcohol-Related Intimate Partner Violence among White, Black, and Hispanic Couples in the United States *Alcohol Research & Health.*

Raynard, Kington, M.D., Ph.D., Acting NIAAA Director, (year....) and Kendall Bryant, Ph.D., AIDS Coordinator, Chief, Collaborative and Special Health Programs Branch, Office of Collaborative Research Alcohol and AIDS—A Commentary

Singh, KK, Bloom SS, Suchindran CM, Singh BP, Mishra S (2004) "Influence of alcohol use on male sexual behaviour leading to HIV/AIDS in Uttar Pradesh, India", *Paper presented at International Conference on AIDS* Bangkok, Thailand

Stall, R.; Paul, J.P.; Greenwood, G.; et al. Alcohol use, drug use and alcohol-related problems among men who have sex with men: The Urban Men's Health Study. Addiction 96(11):1589–1601, 2001.

Stoner, S.A., W.H. George, L.M. Peters and J. Norris, "Liquid Courage: Alcohol Fosters Risky Sexual Decision-Making in Individuals with Sexual Fears," AIDS and Behavior June 27 (2006) Epub ahead of print.

Straus, M.A., and Smith, C. Violence in Hispanic families in the United States: Incidence rates and structural interpretations. In: Straus, MA., and Gelles, R.J., eds. Physical Violence in American Families: Risk Factors and Adaptations in Violence in 8,145 Families. New Brunswick, NJ: Transactions Books, 1990. pp. 34 1-363.

Sudha Sivaram, DrPH, MPH, Carl A. Latkin, PhD, Suniti Solomon, MD, and David D. Celentano, ScD, 2006, HIV Prevention in India: Focus on Men, Alcohol Use and Social Networks, Harvard Health Policy Review, International, Vol. 7, No. 2)18 (1&2) 67

World Health Organization, Mental Health: Evidence and Research; Department of Mental Health and Sub-stance Dependence., "Alcohol use and sexual risk behaviors across cultures: A 2001-2002 literature review from eight countries," (Geneva, Switzerland: 2002).

CHAPTER

Understanding Knowledge and Determinants of Sexual and Reproductive Rights of Youth

— Manas Ranjan Pradhan

ABSTRACT

Youth in India are at a vulnerable, yet crucial phase of their lives coupled with poor knowledge on matters related to sexuality and reproductive health. The present research that attempts to understand knowledge and determinants of sexual & reproductive rights of youth in Orissa uses a multi-stage sampling design to select the respondents. Both qualitative and quantitative tools have been used for data collection, and the analytical packages like SPSS, and ATLAS ti has been used for the analysis. Informed consent of the youth has been taken into consideration during data collection. The findings are based on the data from eight focus group discussions, 500 individual interviews, and 42 in-depth interviews of rural married youth collected during 2006-07. Smaller percentage of youth has knowledge about various sexual and reproductive rights. There exist sex differences in the knowledge level; young women are in a disadvantageous position. The attributes such as education, mass media exposure and inter-spousal communication on reproductive issues have emerged to possess a positive significant association with comprehensive knowledge and favorable attitude towards sexual and reproductive rights. Additionally, perceived gender role along with other socio-cultural attributes significantly affect the likelihood of any sexual and reproductive rights violation.

Introduction

Youth (15-24 years) who largely define the socio-economic and political future of a population comprise of nearly one-fifth of India's total population (RGI 2001). They are at a vulnerable, yet crucial phase of their lives coupled with poor knowledge on matters related to sexuality and reproductive health. Moreover, their inability, inaccessibility and unwillingness to use family planning and related health services puts them at a significant risk of experiencing negative health consequences (Pradhan and Ram 2007; Verma and Lhungdim 2004; Jejeebhoy and Sebastian 2003; and Collumbien *et al.*, 2001). Sexual and reproductive rights of youth have been recognized as an important issue that needs emphasis from a broader perspective of individual freedom and human right. Specifically, with a purpose to promote and protect sexual and reproductive rights and freedom in all political, economic and cultural system, the internationally agreed upon rights are: right to (1) life; (2) liberty and security of the person; (3) equality and to be free from all forms of discrimination; (4) privacy; (5) freedom of thought; (6) information and education; (7) choose whether or not to marry and found and plan a family; (8) decide whether and when to have children; (9) health care and health protection; (10) the benefit of scientific progress; (11) freedom of assembly and political participation; and (12) be free from torture and ill treatment (IPPF 1996).

Although there is a scarcity of information on indicators of sexual and reproductive right as agreed upon internationally, small-scale studies conducted in different parts of the country show the existence of eve teasing, non-consensual sex, sexual violence within and outside marriage (IIPS and PC 2007; Chaudhuri 2006; Mathew 2005; Khan *et al.*, 2004 and George 2003) and unequal gender relation between the couple (Bal and Mahawar 2005 and Ravindran and Balasubramanian 2004). Das (2006) views India as a country of paradoxes as far as sexual and reproductive rights are concerned and has attributed the credit to the deeply rooted patriarchal society struggling for its survival with modern concepts of gender equality and individual autonomy. The present research attempts to understand knowledge and determinants of sexual & reproductive rights of youth in Orissa.

Data and Methods

The data for the current study have been collected in three phases, *i.e.* the pre-survey qualitative phase, the main survey and post-survey qualitative phase during 2006-07. Both qualitative (focus group discussion and in-depth interview) and quantitative (semi-structured interview schedule) tools have been used for data collection. In the pre-survey qualitative phase, focus group discussions (FGDs) among young men and women have been conducted in some selected villages. The selection of those villages has been done at random in the randomly selected tehsil (administrative unit of the district) for the main survey. The young people for the FGDs have been selected keeping in mind the age, education, and marital duration.

A multi-stage sampling design has been adopted to select the youth for the individual interview. First of all, one district has been selected at random out of the 30 districts of the state. At the second stage, out of the existing tehsils of the district, one tehsil was randomly selected. At the third stage, 20 villages of more than 300 households were selected at random (10 each for men and women). This was followed by complete house listing of all 20 selected villages. During house listing, information about sex and marital status of the persons aged 15-29 years had been collected to identify the households having eligible youth for the main survey. From the new list, 30 households from each village were selected using circular systematic random sampling. In the post-survey qualitative phase, for the in-depth interviews (IDIs) a few of the young people have been selected purposively from the young people of the main survey.

More specifically, the findings of the present study are based on the data from eight FGDs (four each among men and women), 500 individual interviews (250 each of men and women), and 42 IDIs (20 men and 22 women) of rural married young people in the state of Orissa. The young men included in the study are in between 20-29 years while the young women are in between 15-24 years. It is worth mentioning that necessary ethical guidelines like informed consent of the young people have been taken into consideration during data collection. The quantitative data has been analyzed using the Statistical Package for Social Science (SPSS 15.0). Similarly, the *ATLAS ti* package has been used for analyzing the FGDs and IDIs. Binary logit regression model has been used to understand the determinants of selected sexual and reproductive rights indicator. Besides this, indices such as perceived gender role, decision-making power, mass media exposure, comprehensive knowledge about RTI/STI, inter-spousal communication on SRH issues, and household wealth index have been computed to understand the composite influence of various independent variables on selected dependent variables.

RESULTS AND DISCUSSION

Knowledge/Attitude/Experience of Sexual and Reproductive Rights

The data in Table 2.1 describe the profile of selected indicators of sexual and reproductive rights. Again, selected indicators have been considered for detailed analysis in view of their importance for better sexual and reproductive health of youth.

Right to Life

All persons have the right to life and no woman's life should be put at risk or endangered by reason of pregnancy (IPPF 1996). Table 2.1 reveals that only 34 per cent of the young men and 16 percent of the young women have agreed that a woman has the right to abort a pregnancy whenever she wants. Qualitative data finds that fear of marital discord besides emotional attachment with the fetus reduces the chance of abortion for the young women. To quote a 24 year old housewife,

> *If you ask for abortion without his consent, he (husband) may suspect your character.*

Another 23 year old housewife says,

> *Why to think about abortion. What crime has the unborn child committed?*

Table 2.1 : Percentage of Youth According to their Knowledge, Attitude and Experience of Selected Sexual and Reproductive Rights Indicators

No.	Description of rights	Favourable/agreed/ experienced	
		Men	Women
1	2	3	4
R-1	Right to life		
	a. Attitude towards women seeking abortion due to life threat	46.0	50.8
	b. Attitude towards women's right to abort a pregnancy whenever she wants	34.4	15.6
R-2	Right to liberty and security of the person		
	a. Attitude towards women's right to enjoy sex	46.0	43.6
	b. Attitude towards women's right to say 'no' to husband when she does not want sex	53.2	46.8
	c. Experience of non-consensual sex within marital union	33.6	40.8

1	2	3	4
R-3	Right to equality and to be free from all forms of discrimination		
	a. Justify wife beating due to specific reasons	71.2	57.2
	b. Experience of spousal humiliation	22.8	20.0
	c. Attitude towards young unmarried girl's knowledge about safe abortion	36.8	39.6
R-4	Right to privacy		
	Experience of privacy in treatment seeking#	48.1	51.6
R-5	Right to freedom of thought		
	Attitude towards women's right to choose contraceptive of her choice	38.0	34.4
R-6	Right to information and education		
	a. Correct knowledge of all modern spacing methods	36.8	31.6
	b. Awareness of possible contra-indications* by health providers	38.6	34.6
	c. Knowledge about the places to get condom	79.6	58.8
	d. Knowledge about the places to avail abortion	76.0	56.0
R-7	Right to choose whether or not to marry and find and plan a family		
	Consulted about age at marriage	49.6	29.6

1	2	3	4
R-8	Right to decide whether and when to have children		
	a. Couple jointly should decide the number of children to have	77.6	67.2
	b. Couple jointly should decide the spacing between children	76.4	69.2
	c. Couple jointly should decide the sex composition of children	83.2	69.2
	d. Couple jointly have decided the contraceptive method used*	70.1	55.3
R-9	Right to health care and health protection		
	Use of traditional unsafe methods of treatment	14.8	19.6
R-10	Right to the benefit of scientific progress		
	Correct knowledge about emergency contraceptive pills	8.0	8.4
R-11	Right to freedom of assembly and political participation		
	Participation in organized groups/societies	35.6	14.0
R-12	Right to be free from torture and ill treatment		
	Experience of sexual abuse outside marriage	12.8	36.4
	Number of youth	250	250

Based on those sought treatment for any RTI/STI

* Based on those youth ever used any contraceptive method

The data further reveal that 46 per cent of the young men and 51 per cent of the young women agreed to the statement that 'a woman should go for abortion if her life is at threat because of pregnancy'. It has emerged from the qualitative data that young people do not view pregnancy as a risk for a woman. Simultaneously, it has been found that the desire for motherhood, which enhances young woman's status in the society, leads many to conceive and carry a pregnancy till the full even in risky conditions. In the words of a 23 year old housewife,

> *I do not know how pregnancy is a threat to life. Anyway you have to take the risk to give birth to a child. Only then you can improve your status in the society.*

Right to Liberty and Security of the Person

All persons have the right to be free to enjoy and control their sexual and reproductive life, having due regard to the rights of others (IPPF 1996). Analysis however shows that irrespective of sex, a little less than half of the youth opined that a woman has the right to enjoy sex (Table 2.1). Again, only about half of the youth (53 per cent young men and 47 per cent young women) view that a woman can say 'no' to her husband when she does not wish to have sex. Qualitative data finds that women in general believe that they should not deny husband's sexual desire, which may lead to sexual promiscuity among their husbands, domestic violence, and separation. As a 24 year old housewife puts it,

> *If you would say no; he will find another one and might leave you finally.*

Non-consensual sex may be considered as a violation of sexual and reproductive rights of an individual. It is apparent that one-third of the young men reportedly have experienced sex against the will of their respective wives. Qualitative data reveals that many young men consider their respective wives as chattels and unilaterally decide the timing of sex, number and timing of children besides type and timing of contraception. Refusal/disagreement of wife to any such decisions often leads to domestic violence and threat of divorce. To quote a young mother,

> *He does it even while I refuse and threats me to send to my parental home. What can I do, after all I am married to him.*

Thus, it seems that young men behave according to their perceived gender role, which often leads to physical and psychological problems for their respective wives. Young women on the other hand quietly accept all these ill-treatment as they perceive them something that is expected from the marriage.

Right to Equality and to be free from all forms of Discrimination

Sexual and reproductive rights envisage that all persons have the right to protection from all forms of violence caused by reason of their race, colour, sex, language, religion, political or other opinion, national or social origin, property, birth or other status (IIPF 1996). However, it has been found that almost seven out of every 10 young men and six out of every 10 young women have agreed with at least one reason[1] of justifying wife beating (Table 2.1). The possible reason may be the patriarchal social structure, which expects young men to have complete control over the lives of their respective wives.

Young unmarried girls' knowledge about safe abortion seems important from a rights perspective. Analysis however finds that irrespective of sex, about three-fifths of the youth (63 per cent young men and 60 per cent young women) show their disagreement to the statement that 'young unmarried girls should know about safe abortion' (Table 2.1). Qualitative data discloses that many young men are quite apprehensive that knowledge about abortion before marriage might lead to greater indulgence in premarital sexual activities among young women. As one young man opines,

Why does one need to know about abortion, as you are not expected to have sex before marriage?

Similarly, one young woman says:

If you would ask anyone about abortion, he/she might suspect your intention.

Right to Privacy

Privacy and confidentiality while seeking treatment are other important issues that come under the domain of sexual and reproductive rights. However, analysis has clearly brought out that regardless of sex, a sizable number of youth (48 percent young men and 52 per cent young women) who have sought treatment for any RTI/STI, have sought treatment from a source compromising their privacy (Table 2.1). In the words of a 24 year old housewife,

What privacy? Many people are there standing in the queue and his shop (clinic) is a small one.

Right to Freedom of Thought

Sexual and reproductive rights pronounce that all persons have the right to freedom of thought and speech related to their sexual and reproductive lives. Findings however show that more than three-fifth of the youth (62 per cent of young men and 66 per cent of young women) have disagreed with the statement saying 'a woman can choose contraceptive of her choice' (Table 2.1). Findings from qualitative data reveal young men have the view that women are unaware of the available contraceptive methods and hence are not in a position to choose the method most suitable to them. Some others consider contraception as an exclusive right of the man, in view of his responsibility to feed the children and hence expressed that it should not be decided by the woman. As an illiterate laborer aged 28 years puts it,

After all, it is the duty of the man to feed the children. So, all the decision including that about contraception must only be taken by him.

Right to Information and Education

All persons have the right to get full information as to the relative benefits, risks and effectiveness of all methods of fertility regulation and the prevention of unplanned pregnancies (IPPF 1996). The health providers are expected to inform the eligible couples about available contraceptive methods and the risks as well as benefits of the methods. Exploring youth's correct knowledge about all modern spacing methods[2], it has been found that merely 37 per cent of the young men and 32 per cent of the young women have correct knowledge (Table 2.1). This has been compounded by the fact that only 39 per cent of the young men and 35 per cent of the young women, ever using any contraceptive method, have knowledge about the possible health problems that may arise after adopting the specific method, putting a question mark on the quality of services provided by the government. Qualitative data reveals that many a time gender role of sexual submissiveness, and a society that still considers exposure to sex and sexual matters a taboo, especially for the young women, hinders women's knowledge about contraception. In the words of a young housewife,

> *I was not aware of any contraceptive method before marriage. Anyway, one does not have to ask anyone about this as unmarried girls do not need them.*

Access to health care services and/or information, counseling or services related to sexual or reproductive health comes under the purview of sexual and reproductive rights. However, information in table 1 shows that one-fifth of the young men and about two-fifths of the young women do not know the places to get condom.

Right to Choose Whether or not to Marry and Found and Plan a Family

All persons have the right to protection against a requirement to marry without that person's full, free and informed consent (IPPF 1996). The data in Table 2.1 depicts that five out of every 10 young men were consulted about timing of their marriage while the same figure is three out of every 10 incase of the young women, indicating the discrimination against girls. The findings from qualitative data reveal that many a time parents and relatives select the bride/bride groom and the youth are expected to accept the selection. The situation worsens in case of young women, as their inability to protest against the decision of the elders often put them at the risk of marriage at the time, against their will. To quote one 22-year old housewife,

> *I saw my husband on the fourth day after our marriage when we performed the rituals together. My parents only chose him and nobody bothered to even consult me.*

Right to Decide whether and when to have Children

All persons have the right to decide whether and when to have children and also to choose and use a method of protection against unplanned pregnancy which is safe and acceptable to them (IPPF 1996). The data in Table 2.1 portrays that more than three-fourths of the young men (78 percent) and more than three-fifths of the young women (67 percent) have opined the decision regarding the number of children should be taken by the couple jointly. An almost similar picture may be seen so far as the decision-making about spacing between the children and sex composition of the children is concerned. Qualitative data reveal that the poor status of the young women in the household leads them to think like that. In the words of a 23 year old housewife,

> *They (husband and in-laws) should decide these matters (number of children); otherwise they would blame you if anything goes wrong in future.*

Decision-making regarding the contraceptive method to be used comes under the ambit of sexual and reproductive rights. Table 2.1 finds 70 percent of the young men and 55 percent of the young women revealing that the contraceptive method ever used by them was a joint selection of the couple. About two-fifths of the young women (39 percent) have further revealed that their respective husbands decided the method alone (table not shown). Qualitative analysis finds that although many youth have reported it as a joint decision, in reality, it is mainly the husband who decides the methods to be used owing to women's poor awareness of the available methods as well as bargaining power in spousal communications. In the words of a young housewife,

> *I was not aware of any contraceptive method before I got married. After the birth of our first child, my husband told me to take pills and I started taking it.*

Right to Health Care and Health Protection

All persons, and in particular the girl child and women, have the right to protection from traditional practices which are harmful to health (IPPF 1996). The data in Table 2.1 reveals that about 15 percent of the young men and 20 per cent of the young women have ever been forced or persuaded for any traditional method of treatment, which may not be good for their sexual and reproductive health. Qualitative data finds that superstition, force/persuasion of the friends as well as family, coupled with incorrect knowledge leads youth to adopt these treatments. To quote a 28-year old male, experiencing involuntary loss of semen,

> *One of my friends suggested me to worship Lord Shiva with water. After following his suggestions, my problem got cured.*

Right to the Benefit of Scientific Progress

All persons shall have the benefit of and access to available reproductive health care technology, including that related to infertility, contraception and abortion, where to withhold access to such technology would have harmful effects on health and well-being (IPPF 1996). However, the analysis portrays that irrespective of sex, less than 10 percent of the youth have the correct knowledge about emergency contraceptive pills[3] (Table 2.1). Knowledge of emergency contraceptive pills seems important in view of the increasing number of unintended pregnancies, especially among the young people.

Right to Freedom of Assembly and Political Participation

All persons have the right to assemble and to canvass for sexual and reproductive health and rights (IPPF 1996). The data in Table 2.1 reveals that merely 36 percent of the young men and 14 per cent of the young women interviewed in this study participate in organized groups/societies. Participation in these groups has been considered as a platform to discuss the organizational activities and issues important for sexual and reproductive health, especially for young women. Participation in these groups/societies may open an avenue for the young women to mix with other people and share knowledge as well as experiences, which undoubtedly is helpful for achieving the sexual and reproductive rights.

Right to be Free from Torture and Ill-treatment

All persons have the right to protection from rape, sexual assault, sexual abuse and sexual harassment (IPPF 1996). However, sexual abuse is not something new to the study population. Table 2.1 has clarified that about 36 per cent of the young women in the study area have ever experienced any sexual abuse[4] outside their marital union. The same figure is 13 per cent in case of the young men.

Determinants of Sexual and Reproductive Rights

The data in Table 2.2 provides the odds ratio from logistic regression assessing the association between the youth's comprehensive knowledge[5] about sexual and reproductive rights (SRR), favorable attitude[6] towards sexual and reproductive rights, and experience of any sexual and reproductive rights violation[7] with selected background characteristics. It has been found that after controlling the effects of other variables (perceived gender role, couple's education, mass media exposure, inter spousal communication on RH issues, caste and household wealth index), the likelihood of comprehensive knowledge about SRR is significantly low among the young women compared to the young men. Again, although not statistically significant, the chances of comprehensive knowledge about SRR are high among youth with a high equitable gender role than those with a low/moderate equitable gender role. The probability of comprehensive knowledge is again at the higher side among the youth reporting either partner completing 10 or more years of schooling, with full mass media exposure, and with an average/good inter-spousal communication on reproductive issues than their respective counterparts. The association has come out statistically significant as well.

Table 2.2 : Odds Ratio from Logistic Regression Assessing the Association between Comprehensive Knowledge about Sexual and Reproductive Rights (SRR), Favourable Attitude Towards SRR and Experience of any SRR Violation with Selected Background Characteristics of Youth

Background characteristics	Comprehensive knowledge[1] about SRR (Yes=1, No=0) Exp (B)	Favourable attitude[2] towards SRR (Yes=1, No=0) Exp (B)	Experience of any SRR violation[3] (Yes=1, No=0) Exp (B)
1	2	3	4
Sex of the youth			
Male ®			
Female	.360***	.412***	2.107***
Perceived gender role			
Low/moderate equitable ®			
High equitable	1.064	2.867***	.659**
Couple's educational status			
Both have 0-9 years of schooling@ ®			

1	2	3	4
Either have 10 or more years of schooling	9.105***	1.959***	.561**
Mass media exposure			
No/partial exposure ®			
Full exposure	3.326***	2.027**	.592*
Inter-spousal communication on reproductive issues			
Poor ®			
Average/good	2.265**	2.455***	.375***
Caste			
Scheduled caste ®			
Other backward class	1.925	1.224	1.078
General caste#	3.598**	1.556	.745
Household wealth index			
Low ®			
Medium/high	1.493	.681	.807
Constant	.016	.202	3.004

*P< 0.10,
**P< 0.05
***P< 0.01
@Includes non-literates.
#Those who do not come under SC, ST or OBC category.
®Reference category.

The chance of having a favourable attitude towards SRR is significantly low among the young women compared to the young men. Perceived gender role seems to have a significant positive and linear association with favorable attitude towards SRR. As may be seen, the odd of favourable attitude towards SRR is two times higher for the youth with a high equitable gender role than those with a low/moderate equitable gender role. Again, the probability of favorable attitude is significantly high among the youth reporting either partner completing 10 or more years of schooling, those with full mass media exposure, and those with an average/ good inter-spousal communication on reproductive issues than their respective counterparts.

Analysis further shows that the likelihood of experiencing any SRR violation is significantly high among the young women compared to the young men, after controlling the effects of other variables. There emerges an inverse and statistically significant association between perceived gender role of the youth and experience of any SRR violation. A similar kind of picture has also been observed as far as the variables like mass media exposure and inter-spousal communication on reproductive issues with experiences of any SRR violation is concerned. Again, young people reporting either partner with 10 or more years of schooling are less likely to experience any SRR violation compared to those reporting both the partners with fewer than 10 years of schooling.

CONCLUSION

Knowledge about sexual and reproductive rights and exercising them, are vital to the sexual and reproductive wellbeing of the youth. Nevertheless relatively smaller percentage of youth has knowledge about various sexual and reproductive rights. There exist sex differences in the knowledge level; young women are in a disadvantageous position. Additionally, although a considerable percentage of youth have favorable attitude towards the sexual and reproductive rights, especially of the young women, in reality, young men seem to be in a better position, as a sizable number of both young men and women regarded the husband to be the sole decision-maker in many aspects of reproductive health. The attributes such as education, mass media exposure and inter-spousal communication on reproductive issues have emerged to possess a positive significant association with comprehensive knowledge and favorable attitude towards sexual and reproductive rights. Again, perceived gender role, education, exposure to mass media and inter-spousal communication on reproductive issues significantly affect the likelihood of any sexual and reproductive rights violation. Gendered socialization and subsequent internalization as well as adherence of youth towards these expected roles influence their knowledge and attitude towards various indicators of sexual and reproductive rights.

Inadequate knowledge about sexual and reproductive rights besides experience of sexual and reproductive rights violation undermines the health and rights of young people, more so of women. The unequal perceived gender role of youth towards sexual and reproductive rights of women and its strong association with the socio-cultural norms of the society urges focused efforts to intensify information education and communication (IEC) programs for promoting gender equality. Gender sensitive programs at the community level creating awareness on the importance of the rights of the young women, is suggested for a more egalitarian society. Lack of informed choice of contraception further suggests the need for sensitization of the service providers about sexual and reproductive rights of the youth.

Acknowledgements

The author is grateful to the Parkes Foundation, Cambridge for financially assisting the data collection of the survey.

REFERENCES

Bal, A. M. and K, Mahawar. 2005: India needs social support system for her women, *Indian Journal of Medical Research* 121 (3): 205.

Chaudhuri, P. 2006: Sexual harassment in the workplace: experiences of women in the health sector, Health and Population Innovation Fellowship Programme, *Working Paper Number* 1, Population Council: New Delhi.

Collumbien, M. B, Das and N, Bohidar. 2001: Male Sexual Debut in Orissa, India: Context, Partners and Differentials, *Asia Pacific Population Journal* 16(2): 211-224.

Das, A .2006: Reproductive and Sexual Rights: History and Contemporary Challenges, *The Journal of Family Welfare* 52 (Special Issues): 19-24.

George, A. 2003. Newly married adolescent women: experiences from case studies in urban India. In S. Bott, S. Jejeebhoy, I. Shah and C. Puri, eds., *Towards Adulthood: Exploring the Sexual and Reproductive Health of Adolescent in South Asia*, pp. 67-70. WHO: Geneva.

IIPS. 2007: International Institute for Population Sciences (IIPS) and Population Council, Fact Sheet Maharashtra (Provisional Data), *Youth in India: Situation and Needs Study 2006-07*, Mumbai: IIPS, 2007.

IPPF. 1996: International Planned Parenthood Federation, IPPF Charter on Sexual and Reproductive Rights: Vision 2000, London: IPPF, 1996.

Jejeebhoy, S. and M, Sebastian. 2003: *Actions that Protect: Promoting Sexual and Reproductive health and choice among Young People in India.* Population Council: New Delhi.

Khan, M. E. S, Barge. H, Sadhwani. G, Kale and J, Sharma. 2004: *Reflection on marriage and sexuality: Experience of newly married men and women in Gujarat, India,* Centre for Operation Research and Training, Vadodara, India.

Mathew, K.M.P. 2005: *Attitudes of adolescent students in Thiruvantaapuram towards gender, sexuality, sexual and reproductive health and rights.* Achutha Menon Centre for Health Science Studies: Trivandrum.

Pradhan, M and U, Ram. 2007: Identifying contexts and vulnerability of the urban youth towards premarital sex: evidences from Puri, Orissa, *Indian Journal of Youth Affairs* 11(2), 105-114.

Ravindran, S and P,Balasubramanian .2004: Yes' to Abortion but 'No' to Sexual Rights: The Paradoxical Reality of Married Women in Rural Tamil Nadu, *India, Reproductive Health Matters* 12 (23): 88-99.

Registrar General of India. 2001: *Socio-cultural Tables of India*, New Delhi: RGI.

Verma, R and H, Lhungdim. 2004. Sexuality and Sexual Behaviour in Rural India: Evidences from a Five State Study. In R. Verma, P. Pelto, S. Schensul and A. Joshi, eds., *Sexuality in the age of Aids: Contemporary perspectives from communities in India*, New Delhi: Sage Publications.

NOTES

1. Includes: (a) if he suspects her of being unfaithful, (b) If her natal family does not give expected money/ jewellery /other expected items, (c) If she shows disrespect for in-laws, (d) If she goes out without telling him, (e) If she neglects the house or children, (f) If she does not cook food properly, (g) If she disagrees with husband's opinion, and (h) If she refuses to have sexual relations with him.
2. Includes: (1) knowledge that oral pills should be taken every day; (2) knowledge that (a) one condom will be used for only one sexual intercourse; (b) knowledge that condom prevent the persons from acquiring RTI/STI from affected persons; (c) knowledge that condom prevent the persons from acquiring HIV/AIDS from affected persons; and (3) knowledge that copper-T can be placed in women's uterus.
3. It includes knowledge that emergency contraceptive pills should be taken within three days or 72 hours of unprotected sexual intercourse.
4. It includes (1) experience of sexual comments towards the respondent that he/she does not like; (2) experience of kissing/ hugging in a sexual way that he/she does not like; (3) experience of somebody touching the private parts/made the respondent touch his/her private parts without the respondent's consent; and (4) experience of attempts to have sexual intercourse with the respondent using force/threat.
5. It includes (1) comprehensive knowledge about pregnancy; (2) knowledge about places to avail abortion services; and (3) correct knowledge about all modern spacing contraceptive methods.
6. It includes attitude towards the statements (1) one should go for abortion if mother's life is at threat because of pregnancy; (2) a woman has the right to abort a pregnancy whenever she wants; (3) a woman has the right to enjoy sex; (4) a woman can say 'no' to husband when she does not want sex; (5) young unmarried girls should know about safe abortion practices; (6) a woman can choose contraceptive of her choice; and (7) husband is justified beating wife on certain grounds.
7. It includes (1) experience of non-consensual marital sex; or (2) experience of domestic violence; or (3) use of any traditional unsafe method of treatment.

CHAPTER

Levels, Trends and Determinants of Early Neonatal Mortality in India and Some Selected States

— Dr. Chander Shekhar and Binod Bihari Jena

ABSTRACT

Currently in India two-thirds of infant deaths are comprised of neonates most of who die within the first week of life i.e., in the early neonatal period. Therefore any further reduction in infant morality can only be possible through reducing early neonatal deaths. Hence it is very important to focus the crucial first six days of life in order to meet the fourths Millennium Development Goal of child survival. This paper examines the level, trends and differentials in early neonatal mortality(ENMR) in India and three states UP, MP and Orissa where IMR is substantially high. It also examines the distributional pattern of deaths during the early neonatal period in the three round of NFHS and regression analysis shows that factors like caste, religion, education, mother's child bearing pattern, ANC visit, and place of delivery and child characteristics like sex of the child, type of birth and birth size have significant effect on the survival of infants during the early neonatal period.

Introduction

High mortality among children in many parts of the world has led to identifying reduction of under five and infant mortality to two-thirds by 2015 as one of the millennium development goals. Therefore, the two indicators of child mortality become common while measuring progress in child well-being in any country. Moreover except some suggestions, MDG document does not provide any specific guideline to the countries. In consequence, many countries set the goals without much understanding the relationship among the mortality risks to the children at different ages. In addition, it is critical to measure the programme in these countries where most of the deaths under age five occurred during infancy. As per WHO (1991) IMR is an accepted global indicator of the state of public environmental sanitation of a community and its importance become more as it affects the desired family size also.

The IMR in India is continued to remain high as compared to all developed countries and many of the developing countries. The IMR has gone down from 129 in 1971 to 57 in 2006 indicating a decline of 56 per cent. The decline in IMR is mainly because of the substantial reduction of deaths during the post neo-natal period. Currently more than two-thirds of infant deaths comprised of neonates most of who die within the first week of life, i.e. in the early neonatal period and the highest risk of death is on the first day of life. The proportion of deaths in the early neonatal period has either increased or remained stable over the years. Hence, it is very important to focus the crucial first 6 days of life in order to reduce the share of neonatal deaths in infant mortality to meet the Millennium Development Goal-4 for child survival. The survival of the new born during the first week of life is mainly determined by biological, maternal, socio-economic, environmental, available health infrastructure and prevailing child care practices.

In the past many studies have been undertaken to know the causes and determinants of neonatal and post neonatal mortality. Bourgeois-Pichat in 1964 had highlighted the differences in relative importance of 'endogenous' and 'exogenous' causes of infant mortality in different countries. Exogenous causes of infant mortality relate mainly to the environment and include deaths due to infections and respiratory diseases. Endogenous causes on the other hand include congenital malformations, circumstances of prenatal life and birth process. Exogenous causes predominate in post neonatal phase where as most deaths in the early neonatal period and late neonatal period are mainly the result of endogenous causes. Mosley and Chen (1984) have proposed an analytical framework specifying for the study of child survival in developing countries integrating social and biological factors with proximate determinants. The determinants been categorized in to five major groups, namely; maternal factors, environmental contamination, nutrients deficiency, injury and personal illness control. Kikhela (1989) has given a framework of perinatal mortality which includes early neonatal mortality, where he described various determinants of early neonatal mortally such as socio-economic and cultural factors, mother's habitat and environment, care during pregnancy, delivery and after delivery, mother's nutritional status, child's characteristics at birth and health of child in the 1st week of life. Mortality due to exogenous causes is relatively easier to control than due to endogenous causes. So the decline in infant mortality is attributed to sharply decline in post neonatal deaths that are easily preventable. As a result the share of neonatal mortality in infant mortality has increased with a decreasing IMR. Among the causes, low birth weight is a crucial underlying factor leading to early neonatal deaths. The WHO standards specify babies with a birth weight of less than 2,500 grams as low birth weight babies who are in high risk and needs special care. The primary cause of low birth weight is premature birth (being born before 37 weeks gestation). Being born early means a baby has less time in the mother's uterus to grow and gain weight. Much of a baby's weight is gained during the latter part of pregnancy. Another cause of low birth weight is intrauterine growth restriction (IUGR).

Review of Literature

Reviewing the earlier work it is found that most studies done on perinatal mortality rather than on early neonatal mortality. Studies in early 1970s concludes that children born in India have a high mortality in the early years of life mainly on account of poor socio-economic conditions, age pattern of child bearing and lack of adequate antenatal and post natal care. This mortality is concentrated in the early days of life and particularly in the first week of life after birth (Chandrasekhar, 1959). The underlying causes of late fetal deaths resulting in still births are similar to those of early neonatal deaths (Morris and Heady, 1955). A study conducted by Saksena and Srivastav (1980) using data of from Dufferin Hospital Lucknow during the year 1976-77, found that among the biological factors taken in that study the age of mother at birth, parity, period of gestation, birth weight and sex of the child and among the socio-economic factors, religion and occupation of father are significantly associated with perinatal mortality. The study advocated locating high risk pregnant women in terms of biological and socio-economic and special antenatal and postnatal care providing for reducing the incidence of perinatal mortality. Birth weight is the most important determinant of perinatal and infant mortality and the lowest mortality rates in the first week of life are recorded among new born infants weighing 3.5 kg or more. The maternal age range 25-29 is optimal as regards birth weight, the younger mothers give birth to a greater proportion of low-birth weight babies and therefore the reduction of infant and neonatal mortality has centered upon the reduction of the births weight lower than 2500g (Saugstad, 1981). The caste and education of mother and her demographic factors, variable related to pregnancy and delivery have significant effect on the survival of infants in the first week of life. The result of the study can help in realizing that with the improvement in socio-economic condition, the loss of human life in the first week of life can be reduced to a greater extent (Achyut *et al.*, 1997). Among the causes of death in the early neonatal period, the major causes are low birth-weight, birth asphyxia, bacteria infection and congenital malformation (Chavan, 1992). There were two sets of factors; one relating to mother (like demographic, nutrition, genetic, etc) and the second relating to health seeking behaviour and availability of quality care services were found responsible for neonatal mortality (James and Subramanian, 2004). Spontaneous preterm delivery and intrapartum- related causes (hypertensive disorder) are the most common obstetric events (maternal complications) most likely to contribute to the risk of perinatal deaths in poor and disadvantages population, especially for delivery occurring out side hospital or health care facilities and prematurity was the main cause of early neonatal deaths (62%) (Hany and Guillermo, 2006). Nearly a third of Indian neonates are low birth weight weighing less than 2500g. Over 70 per cent of perinatal deaths, 90 per cent of neonatal deaths and 50 percent of infant deaths occur among low birth weight babies (Paul, 1988). A study in rural Gadchiroli, Maharashtra, India shows that the primary cause of death were sepsis/pneumonias (52.5%), birth asphyxia (20%), prematurity (15%), hypothermia 2.5 percent and other unknown 10 percent (Bang, 2005). With the intervention on the home based neonatal care (HBNC) the neonatal mortality decreased from 62 to 25 in the intervention area which was contributed by the reduction of 24 points in ENMR and of 20 points the Late Neonatal Mortality Rate (LNMR) (Bang and Reddy, 2005). A study to identify the causes of death among newborn babies in rural Bangladesh found that in the case of 122 singleton babies, the major risk factors associated with death were complications during delivery, prematurity, care by an unlicensed 'traditional' healer, and care not being sought for the infants.

Another study was conducted in rural Uttar Pradesh to assess the rates, timing and causes of neonatal deaths and the burden of still births by using verbal autopsy interviews. The study reveals that 71 per cent neonatal death occurred during the first week of life. The primary causes of death on the first day of life i.e. 0-day were birth asphyxia (31%) and preterm birth (26%), and the most frequent causes of death during days (1-6) were preterm birth (30%) and sepsis or pneumonia (25%). So the study highlights the importance of antenatal education for families and promoting preventive care for all newborns by modifying the behaviours of caretakers during and immediately after the birth, such as clean delivery practices, immediate breastfeeding and care seeking for complications. A recent study suggests that improved care of preterm or low infants can substantially improve survival. Early postnatal vitamin-A dosing, promotion of early and exclusive breast feeding, hypothermia prevention and management, including skin to skin care may also reduce mortality and morbidity in low birth weight or preterm neonates (William *et al.*, 2006). Analysis of causes of death shows that 74 per cent of the early neonatal deaths are amenable to interventions. Interventions in terms of dissemination of information regarding simple care to protect the baby from environmental stress, ensuring adequate nutrition and prevent infections. (Shah, 1984). Early success in averting neonatal deaths is possible in settings with high mortality and weak health systems through outreach and family community care, including health education to improve home based newborn care practices, and to improve care seeking. Most neonatal deaths in high-mortality regions are attributable to preventable and behaviorally modifiable causes (Thomas and Hawas, 2007). A recent cluster randomized behavioral intervention study was conducted in some villages of Uttar Pradesh shows that care packages and behavioral education that encouraged improvement in birth preparedness, hygienic delivery, thermal care including skin to skin care, umbilical cord care and breast-feeding resulted 54 per cent reduction in neonatal deaths in the intervention group compared with control group (Saifuddin and Robert, 2008). Simultaneous expansion of clinical care for babies and mothers is essential to achieve the reduction of neonatal mortality needed to meet the Millennium Goals for child survival.

Need for the Study

From the preliminary analysis it is seen that a large portion of infant deaths occurred in neonatal period and again majority of neonatal deaths comes from early neonatal period. Therefore, any reduction in infant and child mortality can only be possible through reducing early neonatal deaths. Because of involvement of biological reasons the reduction in early neonatal deaths remain more challenging. However, providing necessary information on birth preparedness, recognitions of danger sign, educating pregnant women and caretakers about antenatal care, safe delivery practices and home based neonatal care can reduce early neonatal mortality to a large extent. This stimulates to anyone to understand the effect of non-programmable and programmable variables on early neonatal mortality.

Objectives

(*i*) To examine the levels, trends, and differentials in early neonatal mortality and its share in neonatal mortality in India and three selected states

(*ii*) To examine the distributional pattern of deaths in the early neonatal period

(*iii*) To examine the programme and nonprogramme factors affecting early neonatal mortality in India.

Data and Methods

To achieve the first objective SRS estimates during 1971-2006 have been used. The Sample Registration System (SRS) in India is the largest demographic survey in the world covering about 1.3 million households and over 6.8 million populations. It has continued to be the main source of information on fertility and mortality indicators both at the state and national level. The system has a unique feature of dual recording, which involves collection of data through two different procedures viz., continuous enumeration and retrospective half-yearly surveys. The Sample Registration System gives the information on early neonatal mortality from 1995 onwards but for the period 1971-1994 it is estimated indirectly from perinatal mortality rate (PNMR) and still birth rate (SBR). For comparative study of timing of early neonatal deaths by days are analysed from all rounds of NFHS data, and for the analysis of determinants of early neonatal mortality NFHS-3 data is considered. The National Health and Family Survey, (NFHS-3) 2005-06 provides important indicators on family welfare, maternal and child health, and nutrition, family life education , safe injections, adolescent reproductive health and high risk sexual behaviour. It collected information from a nationally representative sample of 109,041 households, 124,385 women age 15-49 and 74,369 men age 15-54 and the sample covers 99 percent of India's population.

For this study, the information on demographic, mother's habitat and environment, socio-economic and vital nutritional information (such as body mass index and hemoglobin level), antenatal, natal and postnatal care and newborn care practices are used. Though NFHS-3 gives information on antenatal, delivery and post natal care from births took place five years before the survey, the analysis period is restricted to last three years preceding the survey to give a current level of early neonatal mortality and to avoid recall lapse and time-dependent covariates. To study the impact of each independent variable on the incidence of early neonatal deaths, bivariate analysis is carried out without controlling over other variables. Binary logistic regression analysis has been done with dichotomous response variable 'early neonatal deaths' (0- No Death, 1- Death) in three different models by adding some new variables in each subsequent model which is divided into program and non-program variables. The main argument behind selecting these three states is that these are the high prevailing states in neonatal mortality where in Orissa and Madhya Pradesh the rate is above 50 and 46 in U.P. (SRS, 2006). These three states also show high level of share of early neonatal deaths to neonatal deaths (approximately 75%).

Variables Selected for the Analysis

The background variables namely, mother's caste, religion, education level, place of residence, working status, father's occupation, wealth index and mass-media exposure are included as independent variables. In addition, toilet facility, drinking water, types of fuel used for cooking are taken as a set of environmental factors. The mother's body mass index, status of ANC visit and care, registration of pregnancy, pregnancy supplement, pregnancy complications, place of delivery, sex of the child, size of child at birth and birth weight, types of birth, birth order, delivery kit, clean blade, baby wiped dry, and pregnancy complication.

Procedure for estimation of ENMR

Early Neonatal Mortality Rate (ENMR)

$$\frac{\text{Deaths of infants in 0-6 days after birth}}{\text{live Births}} \times 1000$$

Early Neonatal Mortality Rate (ENMR)

$$= \frac{\text{PNMR-SBR}}{\text{1000-SBR}} \times 1000$$

Where, PNMR is Perinatal Mortality Rate and SBR is Still Birth Rate. Before estimating ENMR three points moving average of PNMR and SBR is taken to remove any random fluctuation.

RESULTS AND DISCUSSIONS

Trend Analysis of Early Neonatal Mortality

Along with levels, the analysis of trends is important to know the past, current as well as to predict the future scenario of

ENMR and share of ENMR to NMR to suggest remedial policy interventions. Table 3.1 and Table 3.2 show that ENMR is declining over the years in India and as well as in all the three States. In India the percentage decline in ENMR from 1972 to 2006 is just 19 per cent where as among the three states the maximum decline of 40 per cent is observed in U.P. and Orissa and M.P. stand at approximately 16 per cent. As far as the trends in ENMR of India is concerned it is clear that up to the year 1976 there was an increasing trend and thereafter it started declining consistently. Also the levels of ENMR of all the three states remain above the national average except in the period (1976-78) where in M.P. and Orissa the rate was little bit lower. In UP up to 1985 the level of ENMR was higher than the national level as well as the rest two states, but after 1985 its level is below the two states but above India. Similarly the Percentage of ENMR to NMR has been increasing over the years with little fluctuations in all the three states and India. Now in India and all the three states it has increased to above 70, implying that among the infants who died in the first 28 days of their life, more than 70 percent died in the first week of life. The superimposition of trends shows that sharing level and rate of change are

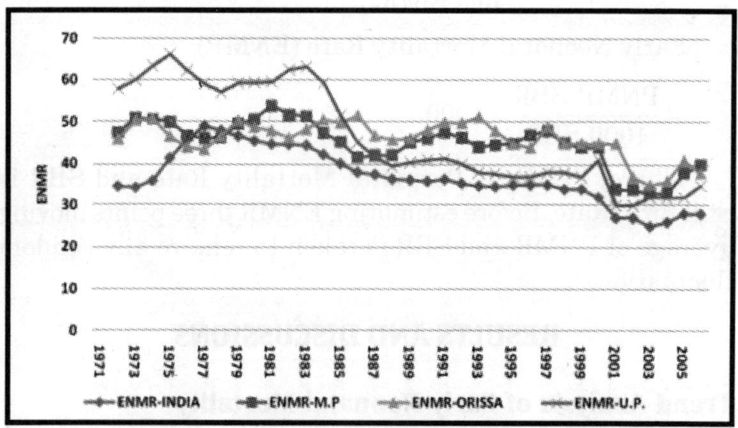

Fig. 3.1 : Trends in ENMR for India, M.P., Orissa, U.P. from 1971-2006

Table 3.1 : Trends in early-neonatal mortality in India, Madhya Pradesh, Orissa and Uttar Pradesh (1971-2006)

Year	Total				Rural				Urban			
	India	MP	Orissa	UP	India	MP	Orissa	UP	India	MP	Orissa	UP
1	2	3	4	5	6	7	8	9	10	11	12	13
1971					-	-	-	-	-	-	-	-
1972	35	47	46	58	37	49	47	61	23	39	29	39
1973	34	51	50	60	36	53	52	63	23	39	26	38
1974	36	51	51	63	38	53	52	67	24	33	29	41
1975	41	50	47	66	46	53	48	69	27	32	25	40
1976	46	47	44	62	51	50	45	65	28	27	25	40
1977	49	46	43	59	55	49	45	61	28	29	23	37
1978	48	46	47	57	52	49	48	59	27	29	23	37
1979	47	50	50	59	51	52	53	62	27	35	23	37
1980	45	51	49	59	49	53	51	62	28	35	24	37
1981	45	54	48	60	48	57	50	63	27	35	24	37
1982	45	52	46	62	48	55	48	67	27	31	26	37

...(Contd.)

1	2	3	4	5	6	7	8	9	10	11	12	13
1983	44	51	48	63	48	55	50	68	28	31	28	39
1984	42	47	51	59	46	51	53	64	26	27	30	35
1985	40	45	50	52	44	49	52	55	25	28	24	32
1986	38	42	52	45	42	45	54	49	23	26	23	27
1987	38	42	47	42	41	45	49	45	23	28	20	26
1988	36	42	46	40	40	45	48	43	22	27	23	22
1989	36	45	46	40	39	48	48	44	22	28	26	23
1990	36	46	48	41	39	50	50	44	22	27	30	26
1991	36	47	50	41	39	51	51	43	24	29	33	31
1992	35	46	50	40	38	49	51	41	23	31	34	33
1993	35	44	51	38	38	47	53	39	23	30	33	31
1994	35	45	48	38	38	47	50	39	23	31	27	29
1995	35	45	45	37	37	47	47	39	23	31	26	26
1996	35	47	44	37	37	48	45	39	23	36	31	27
1997	35	48	49	38	38	51	52	40	20	24	23	23

1	2	3	4	5	6	7	8	9	10	11	12	13
1998	34	45	45	38	37	45	47	40	22	41	24	24
1999	34	44	45	37	37	45	47	40	22	41	24	24
2000	32	44	45	41	35	46	47	43	19	32	27	29
2001	27	34	45	30	30	37	48	32	17	18	16	19
2002	27	34	37	30	29	34	40	31	16	29	18	20
2003	25	33	35	32	28	35	37	35	12	23	18	13
2004	26	33	36	32	29	35	38	35	14	24	17	15
2005	28	38	41	32	31	40	44	35	16	28	15	18
2006	28	40	38	35	32	42	41	38	16	31	15	18

Source: Sample Registration System: Register General of India

Table 3.2 : Share of early neonatal mortality to neonatal mortality

Year	ENMR				NMR				Percent Share of ENMR to NMR			
	India	MP	Orissa	UP	India	MP	Orissa	UP	India	MP	Orissa	UP
1	2	3	4	5	6	7	8	9	10	11	12	13
1971	-	-	-	-	75	69	71	99		-	-	-
1972	35	47	46	58	72	83	75	95	48	58	51	61
1973	34	51	50	60	68	72	81	93	50	71	62	65
1974	36	51	51	63	70	78	84	94	51	65	60	67
1975	41	50	47	66	78	83	85	101	53	60	55	66
1976	46	47	44	62	77	75	79	102	59	62	56	61
1977	49	46	43	59	80	75	77	91	61	62	57	65
1978	48	46	47	57	77	82	72	100	62	56	65	57
1979	47	50	50	59	72	78	82	91	65	64	62	65
1980	45	51	49	59	69	85	88	92	66	60	55	65
1981	45	54	48	60	70	81	80	96	64	67	60	62
1982	45	52	46	62	67	75	76	94	67	69	61	66

1	2	3	4	5	6	7	8	9	10	11	12	13
1983	44	51	48	63	67	76	81	104	66	68	60	61
1984	42	47	51	59	66	79	77	94	64	60	66	63
1985	40	45	50	52	60	68	89	87	67	67	56	59
1986	38	42	52	45	60	66	72	78	64	63	71	58
1987	38	42	47	42	58	66	86	71	65	64	54	58
1988	36	42	46	40	57	73	71	69	64	58	65	57
1989	36	45	46	40	56	67	76	69	64	67	61	59
1990	36	46	48	41	53	72	79	65	68	64	61	63
1991	36	47	50	41	51	68	75	64	71	70	67	64
1992	35	46	50	40	50	64	73	57	71	72	68	70
1993	35	44	51	38	47	65	78	57	74	68	66	67
1994	35	45	48	38	48	60	71	53	72	74	68	71
1995	35	45	45	37	48	65	62	52	73	69	72	71
1996	35	47	44	37	47	64	64	51	74	73	69	73
1997	35	48	49	38	46	64	63	51	76	75	78	75

...(Contd.)

1	2	3	4	5	6	7	8	9	10	11	12	13
1998	34	45	45	38	45	61	60	52	76	74	75	73
1999	34	44	45	37	45	61	61	52	76	72	74	71
2000	32	44	45	41	44	59	61	53	73	75	74	77
2001	27	34	45	30	40	53	59	47	68	64	76	64
2002	27	34	37	30	40	51	53	47	68	67	70	64
2003	25	33	35	32	37	50	47	48	68	66	74	67
2004	26	33	36	32	37	50	49	50	70	66	73	64
2005	28	38	41	32	37	51	53	45	76	75	77	71
2006	28	40	38	35	37	51	52	46	76	78	73	76

Source: Sample Registration System: Register General of India

more or less same. In 1972, the share was just 48 percent but it has reached to 76 percent in 2006 for the country as a whole. The share in M.P., Orissa and UP in measured at 78, 73 and 76 percent in 2006.

A wide gap between rural and urban estimates of ENMR is found. In India residential differentials matter for every socio-economic, demographic and health related indicators as more than 70 per cent population still remain in villages. This may be due to differences in socio-economic and health infrastructure facilities. In India, after 1977 the level of ENMR both in urban and rural areas is declining continuously but the gap has not been reduced significantly. The level of ENMR in rural areas is little more than one and half times to urban areas. The rate of decline in the level of ENMR is more in U.P. in both areas but during the period 1992-2002 the gap had reducing slightly but after 2002 once again it has increased. In the case of M.P. the gap is narrowing down from 1998 but the levels in both areas is increasing in the later part. In case of Orissa the trends are fluctuating with no sign of any reduction in the level of ENMR in both

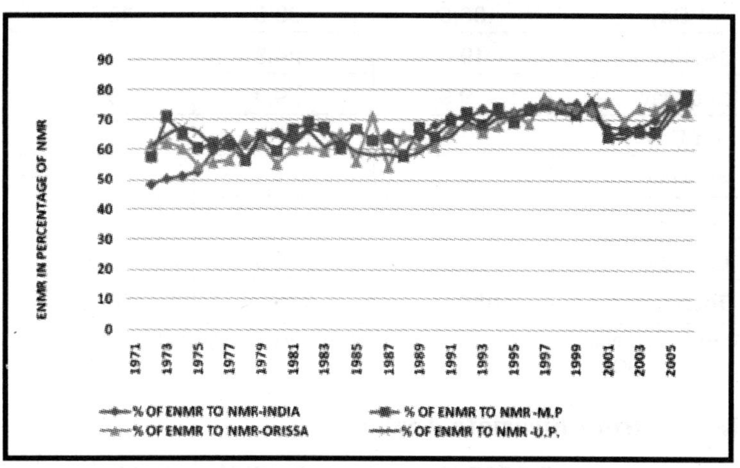

Fig. 3.2 : Share of ENMR to NMR for India, M.P., Orissa and U.P. (1971-2006)

rural and urban areas till 1997 and after that there is decline but through out the period the gap remains more or less constant. The percentage of ENMR to NMR has increased to above 70 in all cases except urban area of Orissa and Uttar Pradesh.

Table 3.3 presents the deaths are not evenly distributed in the early neonatal period. It is clear that the maximum deaths occur within 24 hours of life of newborns. In NFHS-1 the share was 37 percent and has declined to 34 percent in NFHS-2. Further increased to 39 percent in NFHS-3. The deaths in first 48 hours have increased in all three rounds. From NFHS-1 to NFHS-3 the share has increased from 56 percent to 64 percent. If we take the first three days, we can see that more than 80 percent deaths occur in this period across the three rounds of survey and the pattern remains more or less same during 1989-2006.

Table 3.3 : Distribution of Deaths in Early Neonatal Period During NFHS-I, II & III

Age in Days	NFHS-1	NFHS-2	NFHS-3
< 1 Day	36.5	33.5	38.5
1st Day	19.6	24.3	25.8
2nd Day	9.9	9.0	9.7
3rd Day	14.5	1.3	12.1
4th Day	7.5		
5th Day			
6th Day	5.1	6.3	3.9
Total	**1056**	**905**	**774**

Source: National Family Health Survey: Ministry of Health and Family Welfare, GOI

Results from Bivariate Analysis

To know the incidence of early neonatal mortality by different sub-groups of population bivariate analysis is done without having control over other variables. Table 3.4

Table 3.4: Early Neo-natal Mortality Rate by selected variables, NFHS-III Confidence Interval

Non-Programe Variables	Early Neonatal Deaths	Live Births	ENMR	Lower Limit	Upper Limit
1	2	3	4	5	6
Caste of Mother					
Scheduled Castes	161	5418	30	25.2	34.2
Scheduled Tribes	95	4942	19	15.4	23.1
Others	486	18724	26	23.7	26.2
Religion					
Hindu	588	20867	28	25.9	30.4
Muslim	112	5079	22	18	26.1
Others	74	4423	17	12.9	20.5
Place of Residence					
Urban	243	11470	21	18.5	23.8
Rural	531	18932	28	25.7	30.4
Level of Education					
No Education	381	11904	32	28.8	35.2
Primary	129	4333	30	24.7	34.8
Secondary and above	264	14164	19	16.4	20.9

...(Contd.)

1	2	3	4	5	6
Mother's Occupation					
Not working	461	20522	22	20.6	24.7
Primary sector	277	8109	34	30.3	38.3
Service sector	36	1751	21	11	23.5
Father's Occupation					
Primary sector	553	20346	27	24.9	29.4
Service sector	210	9599	22	18.9	24.8
Wealth Index					
Lower quintile	365	10962	33	29.9	36.7
Middle quintile	155	6241	25	21	28.7
Upper quintile	254	13199	19	16.9	21.6
Types of Fuel					
Smoke Free	121	7454	16	13.4	19.1
Not Smoke Free	573	20449	28	25.8	30.3
Mass Media Exposure					
No Exposure	221	7311	30	26.3	34.2
Exposure	553	23091	24	22	25.9

1	2	3	4	5	6
Sex of the Child					
Male	465	15828	29	26.7	32
Female	309	14574	21	18.9	23.5
Type of Birth					
Single	727	29943	24	22.5	26
Multiple	47	459	102	74.6	130.2
Birth Order					
First	317	10008	32	28.2	35.1
Second and Third	272	13489	20	17.8	22.5
Fourth and above	185	6905	27	23	30.6
Child's Birth Weight					
Low (<2500g)	103	4943	21	16.9	24.8
Normal(2500 & above)	65	8092	8	6.1	10
Child's Birth Size					
Small	228	6487	35	30.6	39.6
Normal	491	23423	21	19.9	22.7
Child Bearing Pattern					
Age <19 yrs & >35 years	163	4478	36	30.9	41.8

...(Contd.)

1	2	3	4	5	6
19 yrs <age <35 yrs, BI<19 & BO>1	86	2251	38	30.2	46.1
19 yrs <age <35 yrs, BI>19 & BO>1	298	15541	19	17.1	21.3
19 yrs <age <35 yrs & BO=1	214	7654	28	21.3	31.6
Body Mass Index					
Under weight	270	9598	28	24.8	31.4
Normal	414	16921	24	22.1	26.8
Over weight	63	2607	24	18.3	30.1
Toilet Facilities					
Improved	241	12748	19	16.5	21.3
Not Improved	451	15125	30	27.1	32.5
Sources of Drinking Water					
Improved	561	22924	24	22.6	26.6
Not Improved	131	4979	26	21.9	30.8
ANC Visit					
No visit	122	5213	23	19.2	27.5
1st Trimester	197	13032	15	13	17.2
2nd & 3rd Trimesters	153	8307	18	15.5	21.3

1	2	3	4	5	6
IFA Tablets Taken					
Not taken	168	8458	20	16.8	22.8
Less than 90 days	183	10286	18	15.2	20.3
90 days and more	111	7697	14	11.7	17
Pregnancy Complication					
No	190	11573	16	14.1	18.7
Yes	282	14979	19	16.6	21
Delivery Kit Used					
No	37	1310	28	19.6	37.2
Yes	435	25242	17	15.6	18.8
Baby Wiped Dry and Wrapped					
No	146	7013	21	17.4	24.4
Yes	326	19539	17	14.8	18.4
Place of Delivery					
Non Institutional	424	16109	26	23.8	28.8
Institutional	336	14266	24	21.1	26
Pregnancy Registered withANM					
No	302	14442	21	17.2	22.7

...(Contd.)

1	2	3	4	5	6
Yes	163	12092	13	11.3	15.5
Received Supplement from ICDS					
No	400	21436	19	15.5	19.5
Yes	64	5098	13	9.3	15.8
States					
MP, UP and Orissa	226	6938	33	28.3	36.7
Others	548	23464	23	21.4	25.2

Source: National Family Health Survey: Ministry of Health and Family Welfare, Government of India

reveals the variation of ENMRs along with confidence intervals (95%) across various possible determinants. In the domain of mother's socio-economic and environmental set up the ENMR is highest for those newborns whose mother belongs to SC category (30), lowest for ST category (19) and for others it is (26). The reasons of highest ENMR to mothers of SC may be the fact that due to low socio-economic conditions like, low education and low standard of living. In case of religion it is highest for Hindus (28) and as compared to others it is (20). The ENMR is higher in rural areas (28) than in urban areas because rural areas (21) are generally lagging behind from urban areas in terms of socio-economic and health infrastructure. Increasing mother's level of education has positive impact on the survival of new borns. Among mothers with no education the rate is calculated as 32 early neonatal deaths per thousand live births. While having secondary and higher secondary the rate is estimated 19 per thousand live births. So mother's education has effect on the survival of new born babies. Those mothers who are working in primary sector the risk of dying for their infants are high than non working and working in service sector. The possible reasons may be that those women generally work in agricultural field are neglected to seek health care during pregnancy and delivery. So they are more likely to have low birth weight babies. Father's occupational status is positively associated with the survival of infant's in the early neonatal period. The ENMR is the highest level (33) for mother belonging to lower quintile in comparison to upper quintile (19). Better habitat and environment have also impact on ENMR. ENMR is found to be low among children born mothers exposed to improved toilet facility and cooking fuel.

While analyzing child's characteristics it is found that ENMR was high for male babies (29) and low for female babies (21) which may be for biological causes. The ENMR is found to be exceptionally higher in multiple types of births (102) while 24 per thousand in single tones. A baby whose weight at the time of birth is below 2500 g has greater chance of dying (21) in early neonatal period in comparison to normal babies (8). Small size babies have higher mortality rate (35) than normal size (20) in early neonatal period. Birth order also affects the survival chances in early neonatal period. The first order births and three plus have higher disadvantages over other births. In mother's child bearing pattern the ENMR is highest for the mother whose age is in between 19 and 35 years, birth interval less than 19 months and birth order more than one (38) and the rate is 36 per thousand for mother whose age is either less than 19 years or greater than 35 years. The nutritional status of mother is also linked with early neonatal deaths. Those mothers who had no any antenatal visited the ENMR is 23 where as compared to those visited in 1st trimester (15). Further, those pregnant women who have taken IFA tablets more than 90 days and TT injections, either once or more, the chance of survival of children born to those women is more. Women who faced any complication during pregnancy, the ENMR was higher (31) in comparison to those who didn't have face any of complication (16). The survival chance of neonates in early days of life are analysed by the status of pregnancy registered with the ANM. It is found that early neonatal deaths are less in proportion among those live births that came from registered pregnancy. The reason may be that the non registered pregnant women never get the benefit of antenatal care. The difference in ENMR is not much regarding the place of deliver for example institutional non institutional delivery. During delivery and after delivery new born care practices affect the survival of newborns. At the time of delivery if either disposable kits or a new blade is used in cutting the umbilical cord the chance of survival is more than not using such medical kits. The wiping the baby immediately after may save children from several infections. Immediately wiping the baby after birth increases the chance of survival.

Results from Multivariate Analysis

Logistic regression is applied to show the net effect of each independent variable on the dependent variable in terms of odds ratio, which represents the controlled effect of one unit change in the independent variable on the odds of response variable. Odds ratio of reference category is one, so an odd value less than one indicates a higher chance of survival of infants in the first week of life for any category with respect to the reference category. Here three models are analysed by adding some new set of variables in each subsequent model (Table 3.5).

Table 3.5 : Result of Logistic Model (Odds Ratio) for Early Neonatal Deaths in India (NFHS-III)

Independent Variables	Model-1 Exp.(B)	Model-2 Exp.(B)	Model-3 Exp.(B)
1	2	3	4
Types of Residence			
Urban®			
Rural	1.084	0.974	0.995
Mother's Level of Education			
No Education®			
Primary	1.052	1.343	1.08
Sec. & Higher	0.607***	0.645**	0.611*
Caste of Mother			
SC®			
ST	0.802*	0.368**	0.218**
Others	1.154*	0.977	0.772
Religion of Mother			
Hindu®			
Others	0.749***	0.715	0.609*
Mother's Occupation			
Not working®			

...(Contd.)

1	2	3	4
Primary sector	1.229***	1.756***	1.515*
service sector	1.121	0.767	0.838
Father's Occupation			
Primary sector®			
Service sector	1.015	1.341	1.402
Wealth Index			
Lower quintile®			
Middle quintile	0.875	1.563**	1.525
Upper quintile	0.846	1.563	1.15
Mass Media Exposure			
No Exposure®			
Exposure	1.07	0.714	0.649
Sex of the Child	-		
Male ®			
Female		0.550***	0.533***
Child's Birth Weight	-		
Low (<2500g)®			
Normal		0.599***	0.578**
Child's Birth Size	-		
Abnormal®			
Normal		0.734*	0.680*
Child Bearing Pattern	-		
Age <19 yrs & >35 years®			
19 yrs <age <35 yrs , BI<19 & BO>1		0.9	1.326
19 yrs <age <35 yrs , BI>19 & BO>1		0.586**	0.756
19 yrs <age <35 yrs & BO=1		0.78	0.945
Pregnancy Complication	-		
No®			
Yes		2.005***	1.478**

...(Contd.)

1	2	3	4
ANC Visit	-		
No visit®			
1st trimester			0.441**
2nd and above			0.245***
IFA Tablets Taken	-	-	
Not taken®			
<90 days			1.192
90 & above days			1.157
TT Injection	-	-	
Not taken ®			
Once & more			1.966
Place of Delivery	-	-	
Non Institutional®			
Institutional			3.314***

(0=No and 1= Yes)
®Reference Category
*Significant at 10 % level
**Significant at 5 % level
***Significant at 1 % level

In the first model among the socio-economic variables, caste, religion, education and working status of mother have significant effect on the survival of infants in the early neonatal period. The risk of early neonatal death is 40 percent lower for those infants who were born to mothers belonging to secondary and higher secondary level of education in comparison to no educated mothers. This may be because educated mothers are more aware of antenatal care during pregnancy, about health care utilization and new born care practices. The probability of dying among births to ST category is 20 percent less and 15 percent higher in others categories as compared to SC. The lower chance of dying may be due to the high immunity and biological differences between ST and other social groups. Babies born from mothers belonging to other religion have 25 percent higher chance of survival than mothers of Hindu religion. Babies born to mothers working in the primary sector have higher chances to die in the first week of life. With increase in the wealth index the chance of survival also increases though it not statistically significant.

In the second model we have added variables like, child bearing pattern of mothers, pregnancy complications and child characteristics at birth. The variables which are significant in the first model turn out to be significant in the second stage. All the new variables show significant relationship with early neonatal deaths. Risk of dying is 40 percent less for those babies whose weight at birth was normal in comparison to low weight babies. Among the babies whose birth size was normal at the time of birth the survival chance is 27 per cent more in comparison to abnormal size. Female child has 45 per cent less chance of dying in the first week of life than male child. In the mothers child bearing patterns the risk of dying is 48 per cent lower for those babies who are born to mothers in 19 to 35 years of age group, birth interval more than 19 months and birth order greater than one in comparison to mother having ages below 19 years and above 35 years. Mothers having complication during pregnancy, the risk of early neonatal mortality is two times higher than those women who don't have any complication and is highly significant.

In the third model programmable variables are added to show the impact on early neonatal deaths. The variables included in this model are antenatal visits, tetanus injection, IFA tablets and place of delivery. Mother's child bearing patterns are the only variable which is not significant in this model among those which were significant in earlier model. Among the new variables place of delivery and antenatal visits are significant. The risk of dying is 56 per cent less if mother has ante natal visit in the first trimester in comparison to those who have never visited. Similarly those women who have institutional delivery the chance of dying is three times higher in comparison to those delivered at home. One should interpret the results for institute in the obtained form. For further dissection of data show that there are large number of women who come to institution but never received/taken 90 IFA tablets and did not go for any ANC visits. In contrast, there were a large number of women who delivered child at home but consumed 90 IFA tablets, taken two TT injections and went for ANC visit on or more times. One has to prepare a permutation and combination to create such a variable can reflect the actual behavior along with the efficiency of the program. However, before making such variable one should be aware of number of cases available to analyze further.

Conclusion

Early neonatal mortally plays a vital role in infant and child mortality. Its level has been decreasing since 1971 with slight variation; however the decline is not satisfactory. On the contrary, in case of three states the decline has been fluctuating with large variations. Since the beginning, the ENMR has been above the national average and same is the case now. The share of early neonatal mortality has been increasing in the total neonatal deaths indicating its importance in reduction of IMR. In India the urban-rural differential still persists at large gap though the rate has declined. In case of Orissa the rural urban differentials along with the level of ENMR remains constant over the period.

The distribution of deaths in the early neonatal period is not same for each day. The highest concentration of deaths is within the first twenty four hours of life. This trend has been followed in all the three NFHS rounds. In NFHS-3 the percent deaths within first twenty four hours has increased whereas after day 3rd the share sharply goes down and it is opposite in NFHS-1 and 2.

The study also shows that among the non-programmable factors caste, religion, education and occupation of mother have significant impact on early neonatal mortality. Mothers child bearing pattern, pregnancy complication and child characteristics such as sex of the child, birth and birth size have significant effect on the survival of infants in early neonatal period. Among the programmable factors antenatal care visits and place of delivery have significant effect on early neonatal mortality. Therefore, while developing strategies to reduce the early neonatal mortality these background may be taken into consideration for efficient use of scarce heath resources. The results from this paper clearly suggests that effective implementation of programmes will offset the negative impact of socio-cultural practices on infant and child mortality.

REFERENCES

Achyut, P.; Lahiri, S. and Acharya, R. (1997), "Non-Biological Correlates of Early Neonatal Deaths: Evidences from Five Selected States of India" *Demography India*, vol. 26 (2): 241-60.

Baqui, A.H.; Williams, E.K. and Kumar (2006), "Rates Timing and Causes of Neonatal Deaths in Rural India: Implications for Neonatal Health Programs", *Bulletin of World Health Organization*, 89(9).

Bhutta, Z.A. *et. al.* (2008), "Implementing Community-Based Perinatal Care: Results from A Pilot Study in Rural Pakistan", *Bulletin of World Health Organ*, 86: 452-459.

Bourgeois-Pichat, J., (1964). "Evaluation Recante de la Mortalite nfante'. Cited in U.N., 1973. *The Determinats and Consequences of Population trends*. Vol. 1, new York: U.N.Department of Economics and Social Affairs. pp. 126.

Chandrashekhar, S. (1959), "Infant mortality in India". London: George Allen &Ulwin Ltd.

Chandan, K. (2007), "Perinatal Mortality in India: Trends, Differentials and Determinants", *M. Phil. Term Paper, International Institute for Population Sciences,* Mumbai.

Chavan, Y.S. (1992), "Causes of Early Neonatal Mortality", *Indian Pediatrics,* Vol. 29.

Darmstadt Gary L, Simon, C. (2005), "Evidence Based, Cost Effective Interventions: How Many Newborn Babies Can We Save", *The Lancet,* Vol. 365.

Darmstadt, G.L., Bhutta, Z.A., (2005), "Evidence Based, Cost Effective Interventions: How Many Newborn Babies Can We Save." *Lancet*, Vol. 365: 977-88.

Hany, A.A. and Guillermo, C. (2006), "Causes Of Stillbirths and Early Neonatal Deaths: Data From 7993 Pregnancies in Six Developing Countries". *Bulletin of World Health Organization*, Vol. 84 (9).

International Institute for Population Sciences (1992-93), "National Family Health and Survey-I", *Ministry of Health and Family Welfare*, New Delhi.

International Institute for Population Sciences (1998-99), "National Family Health and Survey-II", *Ministry of Health and Family Welfare*, New Delhi.

International Institute for Population Sciences (2005-06), "National Family Health and Survey-III", *Ministry of Health and Family Welfare*, New Delhi.

James, K.S. and Subramanian, S.V. (2004), "Neonatal Mortality in India: The Role of Maternal Factors", *Demography India,* Vol.33 (2): 157-71.

Kansasa. Zaire "Infant Mortality and Health Studies, Technical Study 61E, *Internation Development Research Center*, Ottawa, Canada.

Morris, J.N., and Heady, J.A. (1955). "Objects and Metods: No. 1 of Scial and Biological Factors in Infant Mortality". *The Lancet.*

Mosley, W. H. and Chen, L.C. (1984). "An Analytical Framwork For the Study of Child Survival in Developing Countries". *A Supliment to Population and Development Review.* 10: 24-45. New York Population Council

Reddy, B.A. (2005), "Home Based Neonatal Care: Summary and Application of the Field Trial in Rural Gadchiroli, Maharashtra, India: 1993-2003", *Journal of Perinatalogy.*

Register General of India (1971-2006), "Sample Registration System".

Saifuddin, A.; Robert, E.B. and Mahendra, B. (2008). "Effect of Community Based Behavior Change Management On Neonatal Mortality in Shivgarh, UP, India: A Cluster-Randomized Controlled Trial", *The Lancet,* Vol.372 (9644): 1151 – 1162.

Saksena, D.N. and Srivastav, J.N. (1980), "Biosocial Correlates of Peri-natal Mortality", *Journal of Biosocial Science*, Vol.12: 69-81.

Saugstad, L.F. (1981), "Weight Of All Births and Infant Mortality." *Journal of Epidemiology and Community Health*, 35, 158-191.

Shah, U. and Pratinidi, A.K. (1984), "Peri-natal mortality in rural India: intervention through primary health care", *Journal of Epidemiology and Community Health*, Vol.38: 138-142.

WHO Collaborative Study Team, (2000), "Effect Of Breastfeeding on Infant and Child Mortality Due to Infectious Diseases in Less Developed Countries Pooled Analysis" *The Lancet*, Vol. 355.

CHAPTER

Implication of Women's Autonomy and Socio-economic Status on Maternal and Child Health in Karnataka

Evidence from NFHS-3

— Sandhya Rani Mahapatro

Introduction

From time immemorial Indian society is patriarchal one implies that the culture of India is highly gender stratified. Women's position is subordinate to man in various household decision making matters. The low status of women in the household indicating the health seeking behaviour of women in such a traditional society is greatly depends on the decision of partner or other elder household members. However, women's autonomy and its association with reproductive health and behaviour have emerged as a focal point of investigations and interventions around the world. Cairo International Conference on Population and Development in 1994, (United Nations 1994), states women's role has been a priority area not only for sustainable development, but also in reproductive health.

A number of studies examine women's autonomy and its relationship with reproductive health outcomes. Increase in women's autonomy will lead to mortality decline and improve health outcomes for women and their children (Caldwell 1986).A study in Uttar Pradesh in North India shows that women's autonomy is the major determinant of maternal health care utilization (Bloom *et al* 2001). The study shows that women with greater freedom of movement are more likely to receive antenatal care and to use delivery care. A study made by Kishor (2000) found women's autonomy to be an important explanatory factor in child survival. Another study in India has shown that women who score greater autonomy are more likely to use antenatal and delivery care for their last birth than women with lower autonomy (Basu 1992). Better health care utilization rates reflected in south Indian women as they have greater autonomy as compared to north Indian (Dyson and Moore 1983).

At the outset, some of the studies used the socio-economic status of women i.e. education and employment as the best predictors of women's autonomy. Safilos-Rothschild (1990) uses women's income as a key indicator of women's status to examine fertility in rural Kenya. Still others (Balk 1994; Tfaily 2004) have used both socio-economic factors and decision-making autonomy indicators and suggest that socio-economic indicators have direct effects as well. Where as Presser and Sen(2000) argue that women's socio-economic indicators such as education and employment are often not sensitive enough to capture the nuances of gender power relations and the ways in which they influence women's and men's reproductive behaviour.

By addressing this paradox, whether the direct indicators of decision making or the indirect indicators are the better predictors of maternal and child health care utilization, an effort is made in this paper to examine the various determinants of women's autonomy and its relation to utilisation of maternal and child health care in the state of Karnataka.

It is stated in various literature that the autonomy of women in a society is largely influenced by their socio-economic characteristics. A woman with higher socio-economic status in terms of better education and employment has more autonomy than illiterate and unemployed women. A study made by (Rammu 1988) in India on Urban, dual and single earning households found that the more resources the partner brought in to marriage, in terms of education, income and occupational status, the more decision making power he/she possessed. He also found that women who were gainfully employed exercised greater authority in all spheres of decision making compared to women engaged in domestic housework only. Basu (2001) stated that female labour supply is both a matter for household decision making and determinant of household balance of power. Women's participation in gainful and visible employment (Women worker in Indian Beedi industry) improvise their bargaining position within the household and is associated with greater gender equality in the distribution of household resources than when women are employed in invisible activities. Female education and labour force participation have been identified as important catalyst for enhancing women's bargaining power (World Bank 2001). Increase in bargaining power of women helps to better utilization of maternal and child health. Besides women's own socio-economic status, education of husband and place of residence also plays significant role in influencing women's autonomy. Education of husband allows women to participate in various decision of household. As compared to rural women, urban women are having more access to outside knowledge and information which influences their bargaining strength within the household so that they participate in the household matters.

It is well documented form the above literature that, socio-economic status of women greatly explain their decision making process. Hence, it can be hypothesize here that like the direct measures, the indirect indicators of women's autonomy also influence maternal and child health care utilization.

Taking in to consideration, the relation between women's autonomy and the reproductive health behaviour of women in relation to various socio-economic characteristics of women, from the literature stated above, the study tries to examine the following aspects.

Objectives

1. To examine the determinants of women's autonomy.
2. To examine the influence of women's decision making indicators on maternal and child health care utilization.
3. To examine whether the direct measures of women's autonomy are important predictors of maternal and child health care.

Basic Concept of Women's Autonomy

Women's autonomy is quite inter-changeable with women's empowerment and women's status. Though widely used in various literatures, there is no single accepted definition that captures the multiple dimensions of women's autonomy. Women's autonomy is a complex and general term with many connotations that is influenced both by women's personal attributes and by the cultural norms of different groups (Makinwa and Jensen 1995).The definition of women's autonomy has been extensively debated and the indicators used for measuring autonomy have consequently evolved (Malhotra *et al* 2002). Autonomy of women can be expressed through various channels like in terms of right to food, health care, education, employment, control over productive resources, decision making power etc. In most studies autonomy has been defined as the capacity to manipulate one's personal environment through control over resources and information in order to make decisions about one's own concerns or about close family members (Basu 1992; Dyson and Moore 1983). The term autonomy as used here following the above definition represented by some selected direct measures, namely freedom of movement to visit families or relatives, decision-making power on making large household and daily purchases etc.

Data and Methodology

Data Source: To fulfil the above stated objectives National Family Health Survey-3 is used here. NFHS-3, a large scale sample survey that was carried out by International Institute for Population Sciences (IIPS) under the aegis of the Government of India; The NFHS-3 covered a sample of over 109,041 sample households, 124,385 women age 15-49. It provides estimates for the country as a whole and all the 29 states. The survey was conducted with the primary objective of providing reliable and comparable estimates of fertility, infant mortality, contraceptive use, reproductive health, family size etc. for different states of India.

The survey also provides information on Women's Status in terms of their socio-economic position. Apart from this NFHS-3 collects data on a large number of indicators of women's empowerment. Information was collected on the magnitude of a wife's earnings relative to her husband's earning, control over the use of one's earning, women's control over resources, wife's participation in household decision making etc.

Methodology: Bivariate analysis and logistic regression is used for the purpose of analysis.

Bivariate analysis is used to carry out the extent of differential in maternal and child health indicators by different dimensions of autonomy and by their socio-economic status.

Logictic Regression Analysis

Logistic regression analysis is used to assess the influence of certain variables on the probability of occurrence of an event. Logistic regression models were first fitted to investigate the influence of socio-economic factors on women's autonomy. We subsequently, fitted two logistic regression models for each of the maternal and child health variables of our study to investigate the effect of women's autonomy on maternal health care seeking behaviour. The first of these latter models includes women's autonomy indicators only, while the second model adds the socio-economic indicators.

DESCRIPTION OF VARIABLES USED IN REGRESSION MODEL

Maternal and Child Health Indicators are

- **Safe Delivery:** Safe delivery is considered as the institutional delivery performed in health institutions.
- **Full immunization**: Children who received one dose each of the BCG and measles Vaccines and three doses each of the DPT and polio vaccines are considered as fully immunized.
- **Ante Natal Care**: Antenatal care seeking behaviour is measured by whether the mother visited medical facility at least three times during pregnancy.

Autonomy Indicators

The degree of women's autonomy reflecting their decision-making capability in various dimension of household matters are assessed in three ways:

- Decision on large household Purchases,
- Decision on daily household Purchases, and
- Decision on Mobility.

The first two indicators on decisions about the two different kinds of purchases (i.e., large and daily ones) were meant to tap into economic decision-making in the household. It is expected decision on economic matter has a significant influence MCH behaviour.

The mobility indicator that is participation in decisions about visits to families, relatives or friends was expected to enhance women's ability to seek and gain knowledge which may influence their own and children's health and well-being. Women whose movement is restricted and where their interaction with relatives or friends is closely monitored by husbands and in-laws are expected to be less knowledgeable about health utilization than other women who have more freedom of movement.

Socio-Economic Indicators

The socio-economic indicators which influence women's autonomy as well as MCH behaviour are as follows:

- Education of women.
- Husband's education.
- Current Work status of women.
- Place of residence.

Education is measured in terms of the highest level of education attained. Three categories have been defined: no education, primary, and secondary or higher education. This categorization applies to both mother's and husband's education.

Current work status of a woman is measured by whether the woman is currently working or not at the time of the interview.

Residence refers to whether the respondent was living in rural or urban areas at the time of the survey.

The analysis of the study is organised as follows:

Section I represents the background profile of the study area. Distribution of women in various maternal and child health by their autonomy and socio-economic characteristics are discussed in Section II. In Section III, various determinants of women's autonomy are analysed. Section IV of the paper examined the separately influence of women's autonomy on MCH and along with socio-economic status its influence on MCH indicators.

SECTION I

Background Profile of the Study Area

Karnataka is a developed southern State of India having diversified culture accounting 52.9 million people which constituted 5.1 per cent of total population of the country. In terms of population it is ninth largest state among the 28 States of India. The demographic profile of the State shows better relative to national average. The geographical location of the State shows that its northern borders lie the States of Maharashtra and Goa; Andhra Pradesh is to the east; Tamil Nadu and Kerala to the south, while the Arabian Sea forms the western boundary. There occurs economic diversification in the State from agriculture to modern industrial economy. Over the last decade, Karnataka's biggest success story is the growth of the information technology-led sector, which today accounts for about 40 per cent of India's software exports. In terms of other economic indicators also the state is well off. The details of the socio-economic indicators of State present in Table 4.1.

Table 4.1 : Socio-Economic and Demographic Characteristics of the States

Variable	Year & Source	Karnataka
Demographic variable		
Total population(million)	Census 2001	52.85
CBR	SRS (2007)	20.1
CDR	SRS (2007)	7.1
TFR	SRS (2007)	2.1
IMR	SRS (2007)	48
Sex ratio	SRS (2007)	917
Social variable		
Literacy	Census 2001	
Male		76.29
Female		57.45
Gender Development Index		0.637
Economic Variables		
GSDP(in crore)	HDR (2005)	61386
Work Participation rate	Census 2001	
Male		64.74
Female		35.26
Human Development Index		0.65

Following this socio-economic and demographic profile, distribution of women in various decision-making matters are shown in the figure 4.1 which is the major concern here.

Figure 4.1 shows the distribution of women's autonomy for the State of Karnataka and India. Decision regarding large household purchases and mobility indices the autonomy of women is higher in Karnataka as compared to other States. Decision taken by the women to purchase large household commodities is around eight per cent in Karnataka which is six per cent in case of India. Like wise to visit friends and relatives, 11 per cent women take their own decision which is around 2 per cent higher than national average. On the other hand in case of daily household purchases, decision of women is low in Karnataka relative to India. The distribution of autonomy indices within Karnataka shows that, decision of women in daily household purchases is higher than other two autonomy indicators. Decision taken jointly is higher in case of visiting friends and relatives while proportion of others is higher in large household purchases.

Table 4.1 : Distribution of Women's Autonomy for the State of Karnataka and India

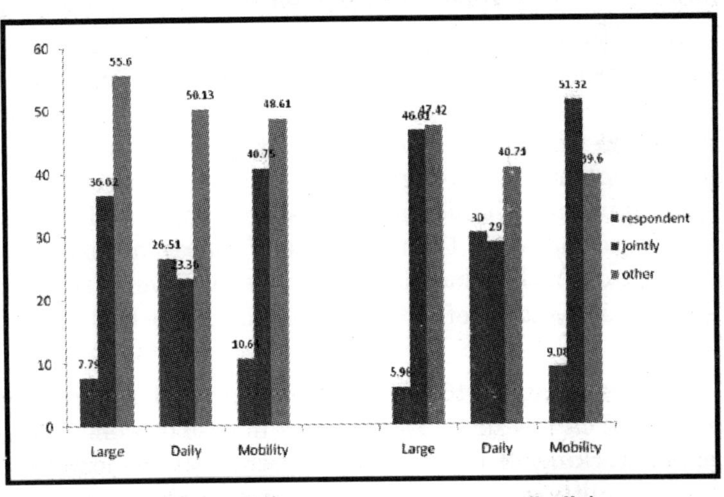

(Karnataka) **(India)**

SECTION II

Distribution of Women in MCH indicator by their Status

Table 4.2 shows distribution of women in three Maternal and Child Health care indicators by their autonomy and socio-economic characteristics.

The bi-variate results of the study shows that, proportion of women taking decision in large household purchases, are found to be low in all the MCH indicators where as women utilising MCH care is higher who takes decision in daily household purchases.

In case of large household purchase more or less 7-8 percent female utilising Maternal and child health while it varies from 27-29 percent in case of women who takes decision on daily household purchases. In case of mobility indicators it ranges from 10-11 percent. For large household purchases other member of the household takes decision as compared to other dimensions of women's autonomy and it is low in case of mobility decision. It is clear from the table that in all indicators of women's autonomy, respondent taking decision alone is quite low as compared to decision taken jointly or by other member of the household.

If one observe the utilisation of maternal and child health care by socio-economic status of women, it is found that maternal and child health care varies directly with education. Proportion of women utilising MCH services are higher among higher educated group. The same pattern is also observed in case of education of husband. Higher education of husband increases the utilisation of maternal and child health care. Unlike education, there exist an inverse relation between utilisation of MCH service and Work status of women.

For instance, 28.46 percent working women going for Ante-natal care while it 71.5 percent in case of women who are not working. It is also same for other MCH indicators. The possibility may be that proportion of female in non-

Table 4.2 : Percent Distribution of Women in Maternal and Child Health Status by Autonomy and Socio-economic Indicators

Indicators	Institutional delivery	Antenatal care	Immu-nization
Autonomy Indicators			
Decision on large household purchase			
Respondent	7	7.14	7.99
Jointly	39.23	38.06	33.47
Others	53.77	54.8	58.54
Decision on daily household purchase			
Respondent	27.36	27.55	29.24
Jointly	23.32	23.66	18.08
Others	49.32	48.79	52.68
Decision on Mobility			
Respondent	10.37	10.41	11.55
Jointly	43.31	42.28	37.26
Others	46.32	47.3	51.19
Socio-economic Indicators			
Maternal education			
No	17.38	22.83	23.44
Primary	12.58	12.11	13.09
Secondary+	70.04	65.07	63.47
Husband's education			
No	18.46	21.00	21.38
Primary	10.42	11.29	12.23
Secondary+	71.11	67.71	66.39
Currently working			
No	76.36	71.54	68.75
Yes	23.64	28.46	31.25
Place of residence			
Urban	46.49	43.58	38.28
Rural	53.51	56.42	61.72

working category is higher compared to working women. The rural-urban distribution of utilisation of MCH services shows that proportion of women utilising maternal and child health service is higher in rural area relative to urban area. As majority of people are living in rural area of the State, hence concentration of women in utilising MCH services is high in rural areas of the state.

SECTION III

Determinants of Women's Autonomy

A large body of literature suggests that there exist a positive relation between decision making indicators and socio-economic status of women. In this section, we try to assess the influence of varies socio-economic factors on women's autonomy.

Table 4.3 presents the estimated results of the regression models (through odds ratio) to examine this relationship in the state of Karnataka. In general, the socio-economic indicators, as measured by women's and husband's education, women's current work (employment), and rural-urban residence appear to be important determinants of women's autonomy.

Maternal education that is women who are in secondary and higher education is positively associated with all dimensions of women's autonomy. In Karnataka, maternal education has a strong positive relationship with all dimensions of women's decision-making domains, where women with higher education are more likely to be involved in decisions on making large and daily household purchases and visiting relatives or friends. Decision making capability of educated women regarding visiting friends and relatives are 2.15 times higher than uneducated women. Like wise in case of economic decision making it is more than one. On the other hand, level of husband's education (both primary and higher) though significant except in daily purchases in the state but it does not improves women's participation in all domains of women's autonomy as compared to uneducated husband.

Table 4.3: Socio-Economic Determinants of Women's Autonomy (Odds Ratio from Regression)

Socio-economic determinants	Women's Involvement in decision to		
	Purchase large items	Purchase daily items	Mobility
Maternal education			
No	1	1	1
Primary	1.36	1.31	1.54
Secondary+	1.97***	1.45***	2.15***
Husband's education			
No	1	1	1
Primary	0.40***	0.96	0.39***
Secondary+	0.36***	0.83	0.48***
Currently working			
No	1	1	1
Yes	1.68***	1.33***	1.7***
Place of residence			
Urban	1	1	1
Rural	0.68**	0.81**	0.74*

*** (<1%) ** (<5%) *(<10%) level of significance.

Further, factors that emerged as significant predictors of women's autonomy are current employment of women and place of residence. Currently working women are more likely to be positively associated with a greater involvement in all dimensions of autonomy in the state. Working women going for large household purchases and visiting friends and relatives are 1.7 times higher than not working women and in case of Ante natal care it 1.3 times higher. This results consistent with the literature stated above that labour force participation of women enhances the bargaining power of women. Women who live in urban areas are also found to be more autonomous than their rural counterparts. Not only women in urban area are greater access to information and knowledge but also the modernisation process occurring in the society affects a lot to their life. This enhances their capabilities to take decision as against their rural counterparts.

SECTION IV

Relationship between Women's Autonomy and their Socio-economic Status on Maternal and Child Health Seeking Behaviour

The analysis in this section focuses on a set of outcome measures that contribute to both maternal and child health: utilization of antenatal care during pregnancy, delivery care at childbirth, and immunization after birth.

Tables 4.4 show the results of logistic regressions with each of the three health care measures as outcomes and with women's autonomy indices and socio-economic indicators as independent variables for the state. Two separate models were run for each of the outcome measures. The first model shows the effect of women's autonomy variables on the health outcomes, while the full model adds the socioeconomic background variables of women to examine whether the effects of the autonomy variables are influenced by the socio-economic variables or they are independent from such influences.

Institutional Delivery and its Relation to Women's Autonomy & Socio-economic Characteristics

From the first models in Table 4.4, it is evident that women's sole final say on mobility and daily household purchases have a strong positive association with the level of institutional delivery obtained. More specifically, women who can make the final decision alone in visiting families or friends and those women taken decision on daily household purchases are more likely to go for institutional delivery than women who do not have a final say (Model 1). Decision taken jointly in large purchase also has significant impact in utilising delivery facilities in both model (1and2). In the full model (Model 2), the other autonomy indicator does not show any significant association with institutional delivery. The socio-economic characteristics like urban residence and high maternal and husband's education all have a positive relationship to institutional delivery. Women who have primary education are three times more likely to go for institutional delivery as compared to women who have no education. With increase in education, the likelihood of women going for safe delivery increases. Like wise higher education of husband increases the likelihood of delivering a child in health care institution. Urban women are also significantly more likely to use safe delivery care than rural women. Unlike other socio-economic indices, the work status of women does not have any significant impact on utilising the institutional delivery facility.

Ante-natal Care and its Relation to Women's Autonomy and Socio-economic Characteristics

In the uncontrolled models (Model 1) which contain only the three indices of women's autonomy, only decision on daily household purchases where decision taken jointly show a significant positive association with the likelihood of using ante natal care. In the full model, no autonomy indicator is significant. The results obtained about the socio-economic characteristics of women in institutional delivery are also same in case of ante natal care. Model-2 shows that both wives and husband's education are associated positively and significantly with the likelihood of safe delivery care. Urban women are also significantly more likely to use ante natal care than rural women. Currently working women does not have any significant impact on utilisation of maternal and child health care services.

Table 4.4 : Determinants of Maternal and Child Health Care Utilisation (Odds Ratio from Logistic Regression)

	Institutional Delivery		Ante-natal care		Immunisation	
	Model 1 (only Autonomy)	Full Model	Model 1 (only Autonomy)	Full Model	Model 1 (only Autonomy)	Full Model
	1	2	3	4	5	6
Autonomy Indicators						
Decision On large household purchase						
Respondent	1	1	1	1		1
Jointly	2.19***	2.01**	0.90	0.69	1.04	0.90
Others	1.35	1.53	1.14	1.10	1.08	1.08
Decision On daily household purchase						
Respondent	1.00		1	1	1	1
Jointly	0.66***	0.73	1.19**	1.42	0.58***	0.63**
Others	0.89	0.86	0.70	0.71	0.77	0.77
Decision on Mobility						
Respondent	1.00		1	1	1	1

	1	2	3	4	5	6
Jointly	0.79	0.70	0.72	0.68	0.60**	0.59**
Others	0.60**	0.65	0.63	0.73	0.68***	0.70
Socio-economic Indicators						
Maternal education						
No	1		1		1	
Primary	3.38***		3.06***		2.14***	
Secondary+	6.23***		4.89***		2.35***	
Husband's education						
No			1		1	
Primary	1.39		1.14		1.28	
Secondary+	1.80***		1.59**		1.43***	
Currently working						
No			1		1	
Yes	0.78		0.88		1.17	
Place of residence						
Urban	1		1		1	
Rural	0.43***		0.41***		1.05	

*** (<1%) ** (<5%) *(<10%) level of significance

Child Immunisation and its Relation to Women's Autonomy & Socio-economic Characteristics

Unlike the other two above indicators in case of child immunization, women who have autonomy on daily household purchase and takes decision to move to friends and relatives has significantly impact on child immunization.

In the first model, women's final say in most of the autonomy indices is positively associated with seeking child immunization. Children of women who have the final say (either jointly with partner/others) in decisions on day-to-day household purchases and of visiting relatives or families are more likely to receive all the necessary vaccinations. In the full model also same pattern is observed. Unlike other MCH indices, in this case not all the socio-economic indicators positively and significantly associated with child immunization. Only education has a significant impact on using the services. That is, the likelihood that the child is getting the full immunization is significantly higher in households where women and husbands have some education. On the other hand, women who are currently working and place of residence does not show any influence on the utilisation of Maternal and child health.

Conclusion

In this chapter the major aim was to examine the relationship between utilisation of maternal and child health care and women's autonomy in relation to various socio-economic indices. Women's autonomy in this study measured by their economic decision making indicator and mobility indicator where the socio-economic indices include, maternal and husband's education, current work status of women and place of residence. The study shows that in large household purchases and in visiting friends and relatives women's autonomy is relatively higher in the state than national average. In the State of Karnataka, large number of women takes decision in daily household purchases as compared to other indices.

The socio-economic factors have significant influence on women's autonomy where women's education, current employment and rural-urban residence being the most important predictors for each dimension of autonomy. These findings are consistent with those of recent studies focusing on the influence of women's socio-economic status on autonomy outcomes (Woldemicael 2007).

The results of the study suggest that not all dimensions of women's autonomy are important predictors of health-seeking behaviour during pregnancy, childbirth, and child immunization. The effects of women's autonomy varied by the health outcomes and some of them lost their significance after the socio-economic indicators are controlled. The most important result from our analyses on health-seeking behaviour is that several socio-economic characteristics, particularly women's and husband's education and place of residence have strong positive association with health-care utilization, implying that these variables have direct effects on the use of health care facilities. On the other hand, For instance, women's sole final say in decisions on visiting families or friends and finale decisions on making day-to-day purchases increases health-care utilization during child birth and child immunization in the state, but not at antenatal care. One of the interesting finding is that women who are currently employed does not have any significant impact on use of MCH services. This implies that women though become the earning member but not have financial autonomy because financial empowerment also requires control over the use of one's own earning. But, it is not correct to hypothesize that financial independence does not have significant impact on using the MCH service. The reason may be that most of the working women are from poorer sections of the society who are not well aware and also not concern of using such services. The current work status may show be significant among the middle and upper middle section of the society. So, one should really look in to the circumstances in which most of the women join in work force.

Then it is possible to find out the exact relation between employment and use of MCH services.

The most relevant conclusion from this study is that in Karnataka though women's autonomy indicators in some cases influence the utilisation of maternal and child health care but health-care seeking behaviours are more strongly affected by socio-economic factors - like education of women and place of residence. Lack of awareness and geographical distance should be the possible reasons for less utilisation of services among the uneducated and rural people. The effects of autonomy indicators are statistically significant in some cases, but most after controlling the socioeconomic indicators, the statistical significance is attenuated or becomes weaker. Hence, in nutshell it can be said that health seeking behaviour of women not only explained by autonomy indices, socio-economic factors play a significant role in utilising Maternal and Child Health services.

REFERENCES

Balk, D. 1994 : Individual and community aspects of women's status and fertility in rural Bangladesh. *Population Studies* 48, 1: 21-45.

Basu, A.M. 1992. *Culture, the Status of Women and Demographic Behaviour Illustrated with the Case of India.* Oxford: Clarendon Press.

Basu,K. 2001. Gender and Say: *A Model of Household Behavior with Endogenously-Determined Balance of Power,* mimeo: Cornell University.

Bloom, S.S., Das Gupta, M. and Wypij, D. 2001: Dimensions of women's autonomy and the influence on maternal health care utilization in a north Indian city. *Demography* 28, 1: 67-78.

Caldwell, J.C. 1986: Routes to Low Mortality in Poor Countries. *Population and Development Review* 12: 171 -220.

Dyson T. and Moore T 1983: On kinship structure, female autonomy, and demographic behaviour in India. *Population and Development Review* 9, 1: 35-54.

Kishor, S. 2000. Empowerment of women in Egypt and links to the survival and health of their infants. In B.Presser and G. Sen ed, *Women's*

Empowerment and Demographic Processes, pp. 119-156, New York: Oxford University Press.

Makinwa P. and Jensen A.1995. *Women's Position and Demographic Change in sub-Saharan Africa.* IUSSP, Liege, Belgique.

Malhotra, A., Schultz, T. P., and Boender, C. 2002: *Measuring women's empowerment as a variable in international development* Washington DC. World Bank.

Presser H. and Sen G. 2000. Women's Empowerment and Demographic Processes: Moving Beyond Cairo. Oxford University Press, UK.

Ramu, G.N. 1988: Wife's Economic Status and Marital Power: A Case of Single and Dual Earner Couples. *Sociological Bulletin* 37:49-69.

Safilios-Rothschild, C.1982: "Female Power, Autonomy and Demographic Change in the Third World." in R.Anker, M. Buvunic, and N. Youssek ed., *Women's Roles and Population Trends in the Third World,* pp. 117-32 . London: Croom Helm.

Tfaily, R. 2004: *Do women with higher autonomy have lower fertility? Evidence from Malaysia, the Philippines and Thailand. Genus.* LXL 2: 7-32.

United Nations ,1994 : *Summary Report of the Program of Action of the International Conference on Population and Development.* New York: United Nations.

Woldemicael, G 2007: "Do women with higher autonomy seek more maternal and child health-care? Evidence from Ethiopia and Eritrea", MPIDR WORKING PAPER WP 2007-035.

World Bank Report, 2001: www.worldbank.org

CHAPTER

Household Environmental Inequality and Health Outcomes of Indian Population

— Ravi Prakash and Praveen Kumar Pathak

ABSTRACT

This paper examines the magnitude of inequality in household environmental condition and associated health outcomes cross different states in India using National Family Health Survey (NFHS-2) 1998-99 data set. The inequality in household environmental status has been measured using a composite index, namely, Household Environmental Standard Index (HESI) by employing Principal Component Analysis (PCA). The extent of inequality in self-reported health outcomes by HESI has been estimated using concentration curve and concentration index. Result indicates substantial differentials in prevalence of diseases across different HESI quintiles and suggests that persons living in the poorer household environmental standards have significantly higher chances of acquiring health risks in India.

Key Words: inequality; environment; household environmental standard index (HESI); health outcomes

Introduction

India is experiencing an alarming situation on environmental fronts and the major environmental problems threatening her society are frightful in their range and severity (Pal 1999).

The result of second National Family Health Survey (1998-99) indicates higher prevalence of communicable and infectious diseases in India. It is estimated that nearly 2468 cases of asthma, 544 cases of tuberculosis, 1361 cases of jaundice and 3697 cases of malaria per 100,000 population is prevalent in the country. According to World Bank (2001) estimate, the premature deaths and illness due to major environmental health risks account for nearly 20 per cent of the total burden of disease in India.

Recent literature have emphasized that poor household environmental quality (HEQ) poses an important public health risk worldwide. Poor HEQ is resultant of biological and chemical contaminants, source of lighting, unsafe drinking-water, sanitation, crowded housing, type of cooking fuel and physical design of household, which causes and exacerbates a variety of adverse health outcomes among household population, ranging from malaria, diarrhea, asthma, sick building syndrome to cancer (Wu *et al.,* 2007). Although, occurrence of infectious diseases depend on variety of disease causing agents, but one can not ignore the influence of individual's neighborhood and household environmental conditions on health status. Moreover, the effect of household environmental hazards on health outcomes may disproportionately vary according to the HEQ i.e. the individual exposed to hazardous household environmental conditions may increasingly fall prey to poor health status than their counterparts. Therefore, this paper seeks to examine the causal relationship between household environmental standard and associated health outcomes in India and major states.

Researchers from less developed countries have tried to examine the relationship between environmental factors and resultant health outcomes in several forms. Mishra and his colleagues (1997) found that use of biomass fuels for cooking substantially increases the risk of tuberculosis among the person aged 30 and above. Salmond (1999) noted statistically significant association between asthma and household environmental condition by place of residence. Rona (1999) pointed out disproportionate increase in asthma among lower social classes and marginal relation to family size. Using NFHS-2 (1998-99) data, Hazra *et al.* (2007) observed that in North-Eastern states, women who either used traditional cooking fuel or had no separate room as kitchen were at 1.3 times higher risk of contracting asthma. An analysis of data on 2,00,000 Indian adults found an association between self-reported tuberculosis and exposure to wood smoke (Mishra et al. 1999). People living in households burning biomass reported tuberculosis more frequently than those using cleaner fuels, with an odds of 2.58 (95% CI: 1.98, 3.37) after adjustment for a range of socio-economic factors. These findings were similar to the study conducted in North India, which reported an association between the use of biomass fuel and tuberculosis defined by clinical measures (Gupta and Mathur, 1997) although adjustment was made only for age.

The influence of poor household environmental condition on the health status of children has also been examined by Audinarayana (2007) and Mishra *et al.* (2005), who concluded that children living in households using biomass fuels for cooking or heating were two times more likely to suffer from acute respiratory infections (ARI) than children in household using cleaner fuels (OR= 1.82; 95% CI: 1.58, 2.09). However, this effect marginally reduces when exposure to environmental tobacco smoke and other factors were statistically controlled (OR=1.58; 95% CI: 1.28, 1.95). Experiences elsewhere also confirmed the notion that poor HEQ plays a pivotal role in determining health status of individual (Mishra 2003; Ezzati and Kammen 2001; Broor et al. 2001).

Investigating the relationship with household environmental quality is although not a new dimension of research, however, the previous attempts have only explored the association between occurrences of specific disease with a particular disease causing agents. One to one relationship between disease and corresponding risk factors may not unravel the overall impact of household environmental condition on associated health outcome. In general, individuals may have exposure to multiple set of disease causing household environmental factors and therefore, it becomes important to examine the combined effects of such risk factors on the health outcomes. To fulfill these lacunae, this paper examines the causal relationship between household environmental condition and health outcomes in general, and understand the effect of inequality in household environmental condition (unequal exposures to household environmental risk factors) and its impact on health outcomes (asthma, tuberculosis and malaria) of individuals at both national, and sub-national level in particular.

Data and Methods

The data from National Family Health Survey (NFHS-2) 1998-99 is used for the analysis purpose. Although the recent data of National Family Health Survey i.e. NFHS-3, 2005-06) is available but the detailed information on health condition of each household member is not collected in the recent round of survey. Keeping this into mind, it was thought to use the data from NFHS-2 which can give the detail information on household environmental status and health condition of each household member. In NFHS-2 information was collected on various economic, demographic, social, environmental and health aspects from a nationally representative sample of 92,486 households. This survey provides a national representative sample with a wide coverage (99 per cent) of country's population. The present analysis is based on 4,84,535 household members. In this survey, few states and categories of households were over-sampled and non-response rates varied from one geographical region to another. To adjust for over-sampling and non-response, weights have been used to maintain the representativeness of the sample.

Response and predictor variables

The prevalence of diseases (asthma, tuberculosis, and malaria) for all household members has been used as response variable. Since asthma and tuberculosis are chronic diseases, survey does not provide any reference period for them, while the reference period for malaria is 12 months prior to the survey date. In order to measure the inequality in household environmental standard a composite index, namely, Household Environmental Standard Index (HESI) has been computed using principal component analysis (PCA). The score of each of the variables entered in the computation of index is given in the appendix. Although, NFHS-2 provides the opportunity to measure the standard of living (SLI) of household by taking account of household assets and consumer durables along with the household environmental variables (as source of drinking water, type of toilet facility, main source of lighting, main cooking fuel, separate rooms used as kitchen and type of house). But SLI is a very crude index based on arbitrary assigned weights and unable to reflect the environmental condition of household. Therefore, to capture the impact of household environmental standard on health outcomes, HESI is constructed based on these six selected household environmental variables. Apart from HESI, some other household level (caste, religion, place of residence, separate kitchen for cooking, and average person per room) and individual level (age, sex, and educational status of household member) predictors are used as control variables.

Method of Analysis

The present study uses the descriptive analysis of health outcomes of individuals according to household environmental standards. The state level variation in the prevalence of various diseases (asthma, tuberculosis and malaria) has been analyzed according to the HESI. The bi-variate analysis is carried out to study the prevalence of disease according to various environmental and socio-demographic characteristics of the household members. The concentration curve (CC) and concentration index (CI) have been used to examine the inequality in health outcomes by different categories of household environmental standards. The binary logistic regression model has been used to assess the effect of inequality in household environmental standard on health outcomes after controlling for other background characteristics.

FINDINGS

Household Environmental Status Across the States

The household environmental standard index (HESI) has been classified into five quintiles ranging from lowest to highest based on weighted scores of household environmental variables. The higher concentration of household population in the lowest quintile is suggestive of highly fragile and vulnerable household environmental condition, whereas concentration of household population in the highest quintile indicates relatively healthier and protective household environmental conditions. Result (Fig. 5.1) shows the mean HESI score and percentage distribution of household population in different HESI quintiles in India and major states during 1998-99. It can be seen that the percentage of household population in highest quintile of HESI was more among those states where mean HESI score was also high. This suggests that the higher mean HESI score indicates relatively better household environmental standard and *vis-à-vis*. Larger concentration of household population in the lowest quintile of HESI was observed in Bihar (44%), Orissa (41.6%), Uttar Pradesh (32.5%) etc. whereas among highest quintile of HESI, higher concentration of population has been found in Gujarat (37.8%), Maharashtra (33.4%), and Punjab (33.2%). This indicates that Bihar, Orissa, Uttar Pradesh, West Bengal etc., comprise group of states where household population were living in environmentally disadvantageous position, compared to the States such as Gujarat, Punjab, Maharashtra, Karnataka etc., where household population is largely concentrated in the higher quintiles which puts them at relatively lower risk of adverse health outcomes because of a healthier environmental condition.

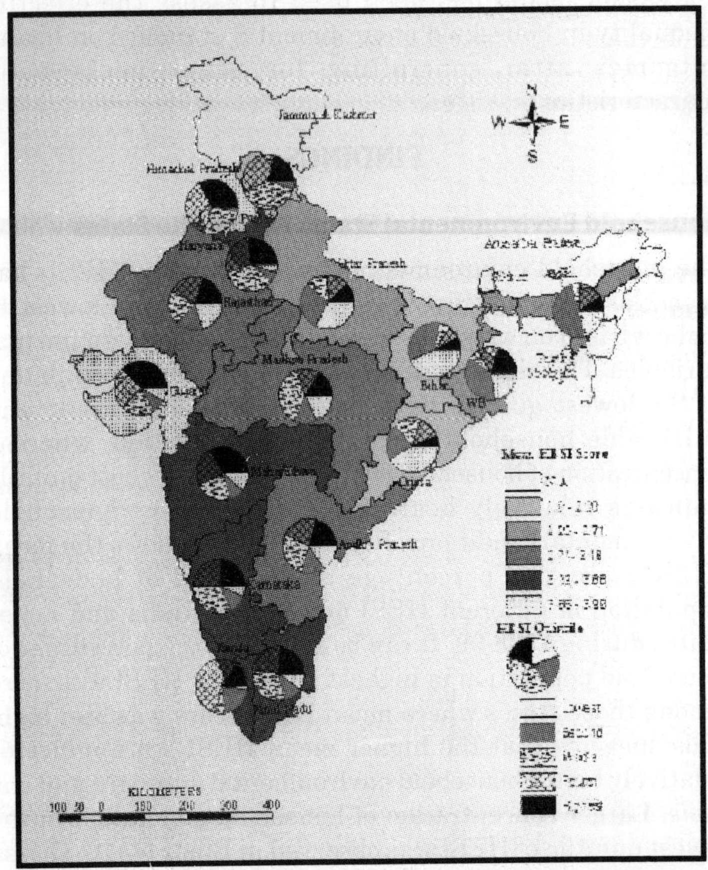

Fig. 5.1 : Mean HESI Score and Distribution of Household Population According to HESI Quintiles in Major Indian States, 1998-99

The effect of household environmental standard on health outcomes substantially varies with the place of residence. Considering the large regional disparities in India, the pattern of morbidity prevalence may not be truly reflected by a simple rural/urban classification which indicates a need for more refined classification of place of residence. Table 5.1 provides the distribution of household members according to household environmental standard and place of residence. The higher proportion of household members residing in countryside belongs to lowest, second and third quintile of HESI. On the contrary, relatively large proportion of fourth and fifth quintile of HESI household members live in large cites, or towns. It depicts relatively poorer household environmental status for household members living in countryside than those living in large cities or towns.

Prevalence of Diseases by HESI among Household Members in Major States of India

Table 5.2 shows the prevalence of asthma, tuberculosis and malaria in India and major states by Household Environmental Standard Index (HESI) during 1998-99. On average, household population belonging to lower quintile of HESI reported higher prevalence of asthma, tuberculosis and malaria than their counterparts. In India, nearly 2.7 per cent of household population belonging to lowest quintile reported asthma cases while 0.7 and 5.6 per cent of them tuberculosis and malaria respectively. On the other hand, the prevalence of asthma (1.8%), tuberculosis (0.2%) and malaria (1.9%) was found to be relatively lower among the population belonging to highest quintile of HESI than otherwise.

There exists a huge state level variation in the prevalence of diseases by HESI. For instance, the prevalence of asthma ranges from 10.2 per cent (Kerala) to 1.5 per cent (Haryana and Tamil Nadu) among the lowest quintile of HESI, whereas it varies from 3.4 per cent (Kerala) to 1.1 per cent (Gujarat) in the highest quintile. The highest prevalence of tuberculosis among population belonging to the lowest and highest quintile of HESI were reported in Kerala (1.3%) and Assam

Table 5.1 : Per cent Distribution of Household Members according to HESI by Place of Residence in India, 1998-99

Household Environmental Standards	Place of residence				Total
	Capital, large city	Small city	Town	Countryside	
Lowest	0.13	0.34	2.74	96.78	79360
Second	0.90	1.43	5.32	92.34	83301
Middle	1.06	1.87	7.92	89.16	93518
Fourth	7.72	7.02	18.26	66.99	108077
Highest	38.56	16.59	26.78	18.07	120279
Total	**11.68**	**6.35**	**13.61**	**68.36**	**484535**

Table 5.2 : Percentage of Household Members Suffering from Asthma, Tuberculosis and Malaria Across Major States of India According to HESI, 1998-99

State/ Regions	Asthma					Tuberculosis					Malaria				
	Lowest	Second	Middle	Fourth	Highest	Lowest	Second	Middle	Fourth	Highest	Lowest	Second	Middle	Fourth	Highest
Andhra Pradesh	5.4	5.1	4.6	3.5	2.9	0.6	0.6	1.0	0.4	0.1	6.3	6.4	5.7	3.8	2.4
Assam	3.3	3.7	2.7	2.6	1.4	0.6	0.9	0.4	0.4	0.5	4.1	3.3	2.0	1.5	0.8
Bihar	2.3	2.0	2.2	1.5	1.5	1.1	1.1	1.0	0.7	0.2	5.2	3.4	2.3	1.7	1.2
Gujarat	2.7	2.9	3.0	2.0	1.1	0.6	0.8	0.8	0.4	0.2	6.9	7.5	5.2	3.9	2.8
Haryana	1.5	2.2	2.0	1.9	1.7	0.4	0.7	0.4	0.4	0.2	3.4	2.6	2.7	1.8	1.0
Himachal Pradesh	NA	0.9	1.5	1.2	1.3	NA	NA	0.3	0.1	0.3	NA	0.9	0.6	0.4	0.2
Karnataka	2.3	2.0	1.8	1.4	1.6	0.2	0.2	0.3	0.3	0.1	1.0	0.5	0.6	0.8	0.2
Kerala	10.2	5.2	6.3	4.6	3.4	1.3	0.8	1.0	0.4	0.1	NA	0.0	0.5	0.0	0.0
Madhya Pradesh	2.6	2.2	2.5	1.8	1.7	0.6	0.6	0.8	0.4	0.3	14.4	11.8	10.3	7.4	5.0
Maharashtra	2.9	2.6	2.7	2.7	1.8	0.1	0.3	0.4	0.2	0.3	5.3	4.1	4.7	4.0	3.1
Orissa	3.1	3.9	3.4	2.8	2.6	1.0	1.0	1.1	0.4	0.3	9.5	7.9	5.9	3.4	3.2
Punjab	1.6	2.0	1.4	1.2	1.3	0.8	0.7	0.2	0.2	0.1	0.8	2.7	0.9	1.1	1.1
Rajasthan	3.5	3.7	3.0	2.7	2.7	0.4	0.3	0.5	0.4	0.3	5.5	4.6	4.4	3.3	3.1
Tamil Nadu	1.5	1.7	1.7	1.6	1.2	0.8	0.8	0.5	0.4	0.2	0.9	0.3	0.3	0.4	0.3
West Bengal	2.0	3.1	2.5	2.4	2.2	0.5	0.8	0.2	0.2	0.2	2.5	1.3	1.1	1.1	1.1
Uttar Pradesh	2.2	2.0	1.8	1.8	1.5	0.6	0.6	0.5	0.6	0.4	4.3	4.4	3.5	2.1	1.2
India	2.7	2.8	2.6	2.4	1.8	0.7	0.7	0.6	0.4	0.2	5.6	4.1	4.3	2.4	1.9

NA: Not available.

(0.3%) respectively. Similarly, Madhya Pradesh (14.4%) and Punjab (0.8%) reported the highest and lowest prevalence of malaria respectively among the population belonging to the lower quintile of HESI. In case of highest quintile too, Madhya Pradesh (5%) remained as the highest prevalence state. This high concentration of disease prevalence in lowest HESI quintile across states indicates that poor household environment may be one of the important reasons of adverse health outcomes.

Prevalence of Diseases among Different HESI Quintiles by Background Characteristics

Table 5.3 shows the percentage of household members reportedly suffering from asthma, tuberculosis and malaria in India by their selected background characteristics. The prevalence of asthma, tuberculosis and malaria varies by the age group of household member across all HESI quintiles. Interestingly, the prevalence of diseases consistently increased with increase in age of the household members within the each quintile, but the magnitude of disease prevalence was relatively lower in the higher quintiles. The prevalence of disease declines as one move from lowest to highest HESI quintile, mainly in older age-groups. The sex-differential in prevalence of disease by HESI is also evident from the analysis, as males were in disadvantageous position to females in lower HESI quintile. However, the females were in relatively disadvantageous position than males in the highest HESI quintile. Educational differential in disease (asthma, tuberculosis and malaria) prevalence by HESI quintiles shows that illiterates were largely suffering from diseases across all quintiles. The availability of separate kitchen in the household shows lesser disease prevalence across HESI quintiles. The prevalence of diseases by place of residence shows that people living in the capital or large cities were suffering relatively more than those living in the towns or countryside across all the HESI quintiles.

Inequality in Disease Prevalence by Concentration Curve and Concentration Index

The concentration curve and concentration index have been used to estimate the inequality in the distributions of various diseases by level of household environmental standards.

It is clear from Fig. 5.2 that concentration curves are above the line of equality indicating that disease prevalence are disproportionately concentrated among the members belonging to the lowest household environmental status (HESI) than their counterparts. The concentration curve for asthma is closest to the line of equality suggesting relatively lesser inequality in the risk of asthma by HESI. However, the higher disproportionate concentration can be seen for tuberculosis followed by malaria suggesting greater inequality in the prevalence of these diseases than asthma by HESI. The concentration index, a summary measure of inequality, shows the higher inequality for tuberculosis (-0.1999) followed by malaria (-0.1991) and asthma (-0.0715). The negative values of the concentration index (CI) exhibits greater vulnerable health outcomes for household members from relatively poorer environmental households.

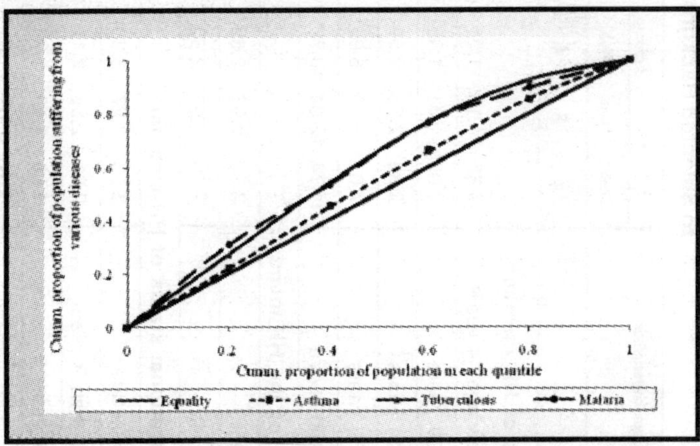

Fig. 5.2 : Inequality in Disease Prevalence by Concentration Curve and Concentration Index in India, 1998-99

Table 5.3 : Percentage of Household Members Suffering from Different Diseases According to Selected Background Characteristics by HESI, India, 1998-99

Background characteristic	Asthma					Tuberculosis					Malaria				
	Lowest	Second	Middle	Fourth	Highest	Lowest	Second	Middle	Fourth	Highest	Lowest	Second	Middle	Fourth	Highest
1	2	3	4	5	6	7	8	9	10	11	12	13	14	15	16
Age of HH members															
Below age 14 years	0.85	1.15	1.01	0.93	0.66	0.14	0.18	0.18	0.15	0.09	5.15	3.57	3.88	2.24	2.01
15-29 years	1.09	1.31	1.08	0.91	0.83	0.54	0.54	0.45	0.25	0.22	5.12	4.10	4.08	2.49	1.83
30-44 years	2.88	2.85	2.59	2.40	1.65	1.33	1.26	0.91	0.56	0.28	6.30	4.42	4.96	2.52	1.98
45-59 years	7.07	5.80	5.95	5.17	3.45	1.72	1.41	1.43	0.73	0.47	6.79	4.36	5.10	2.70	1.73
60 and above	11.74	12.04	10.72	10.14	7.13	1.60	2.00	1.39	1.12	0.54	6.63	5.23	4.90	2.60	1.45
Sex of the HH members															
Male	2.93	2.97	2.69	2.42	1.70	0.82	0.83	0.72	0.47	0.25	5.75	4.21	4.33	2.45	1.84
Female	2.39	2.56	2.50	2.37	1.86	0.58	0.60	0.49	0.32	0.25	5.46	3.89	4.33	2.43	1.91
Educational status of HH members															
Non-literate	3.00	3.27	3.33	3.19	2.08	0.73	0.79	0.64	0.51	0.28	5.47	4.21	4.58	2.79	2.09
Less than 9 years	2.06	2.38	2.11	2.25	1.89	0.62	0.62	0.58	0.37	0.31	5.97	3.81	4.34	2.41	2.05
9-12 years	1.68	1.40	1.28	1.43	1.49	0.72	0.67	0.54	0.29	0.22	5.55	4.10	3.49	2.05	1.67
More than 12 years	0.93	0.98	1.07	1.34	1.66	0.47	0.20	0.72	0.18	0.13	4.91	3.24	2.08	1.46	1.55

1	2	3	4	5	6	7	8	9	10	11	12	13	14	15	16
Average person in the HH															
Less than 2 person	3.59	3.25	3.16	2.71	2.01	0.97	0.79	0.74	0.39	0.18	6.92	4.82	4.41	1.98	1.55
2-4 person	2.62	2.76	2.44	2.27	1.51	0.73	0.64	0.58	0.39	0.30	5.51	3.83	4.06	2.65	2.20
5 or more person	2.30	2.10	2.37	1.91	1.62	0.50	0.84	0.53	0.43	0.42	5.17	3.69	4.99	3.12	2.35
Separate kitchen in the HH															
No	2.67	2.74	2.58	2.36	1.90	0.72	0.77	0.63	0.45	0.53	5.56	4.02	5.01	3.00	2.78
Yes	2.63	2.80	2.61	2.41	1.75	0.55	0.65	0.58	0.37	0.19	5.91	4.09	3.58	2.18	1.67
Religion															
Hindu	2.63	2.60	2.64	2.39	1.79	0.68	0.64	0.62	0.35	0.22	5.60	4.27	4.52	2.60	1.79
Muslim	2.79	3.29	2.16	2.21	1.55	0.81	1.02	0.48	0.56	0.39	3.85	2.58	2.75	1.94	2.24
Other	3.13	3.88	2.50	2.81	2.10	0.88	0.89	0.53	0.46	0.26	11.53	6.33	3.38	2.19	1.90
Caste															
SC/ST	2.52	2.75	2.64	2.10	1.72	0.73	0.80	0.75	0.35	0.40	6.55	5.17	5.37	3.02	2.37
OBC	2.76	2.41	2.59	2.46	1.66	0.77	0.62	0.62	0.40	0.22	5.17	3.82	4.01	2.62	1.67
General	2.82	2.99	2.53	2.36	1.89	0.54	0.68	0.46	0.39	0.24	4.79	3.63	3.76	2.15	1.95
Place of residence															
Capital, large city	3.80	1.91	2.21	1.98	1.74	1.27	1.28	0.92	0.65	0.36	7.59	1.91	3.67	2.89	2.15
Small city	3.55	2.23	3.60	2.05	1.74	1.18	0.45	0.65	0.48	0.24	4.02	2.17	2.70	2.32	1.59
Town	2.34	2.50	2.60	2.03	1.72	0.78	0.97	0.52	0.46	0.17	3.08	3.79	3.22	2.15	1.69
Countryside	2.67	2.79	2.57	2.57	1.97	0.70	0.71	0.61	0.35	0.20	5.68	4.11	4.47	2.51	2.08

Result from Logistic Regression Analysis

The binary logistic regression model has been used to examine the causal effects of environmental characteristics along with the other confounding variables on the risk of disease occurrence. Each of the disease has been taken as a response variable in different models and the result has been shown in Table 5.4. The age and sex of the individual, education, HESI, average person in the household, caste and religion have statistically significant influence on the risk of suffering from asthma among household members. The effect of place of residence on risk of occurrence of asthma was found to be statistically insignificant. However, after controlling for all the individual and household characteristics, HESI plays a statistically significant and negative effect on the risk of contracting asthma, tuberculosis as well as malaria among the members of the higher HESI quintile than the lowest HESI quintile.

After adjusting the effect of different confounding variables, the individuals belonging to households with better environmental condition were significantly less likely to contact with the diseases like asthma (OR=0.735, 95% CI=0.69-0.82), tuberculosis (OR=0.387, 95% CI=0.31-0.48), and malaria (OR=0.506, 95% CI=0.47-0.55) compared to those household members who belonged to relatively adverse household environmental condition.

Discussion and Conclusions

The association between environmental factors and health outcomes has been studied in developing countries for some time, however, the role of inequality in household environment and its influence on health outcomes has been a neglected field of investigation of late. There are studies which have examined the different elements of environment and its impact on health status. However, one can not ignore

Table 5.4 : Adjusted Odds Ratio Assessing Association of Health Outcomes with Household Environmental Standard Index, India, 1998-99

HESI	Health outcomes		
	Asthma	**Tuberculosis**	**Malaria**
Lowest	Ref.	Ref.	Ref.
Second	1.052 (0.99-1.12)	1.092 (0.97-1.23)	0.813[a] (0.77-0.85)
Middle	0.981 (0.92-1.04)	0.964 (0.86-1.08)	0.848[a] (0.81-0.88)
Fourth	0.909[a] (0.85-0.97)	0.600[a] (0.52-0.69)	0.548[a] (0.52-0.58)
Highest	0.753[a] (0.69-0.82)	0.387[a] (0.31-0.48)	0.506[a] (0.47-0.55)

Ref. Reference category. HESI - Household Environmental Health Standard Index. Values in parenthesis represent 95% confidence interval. [a]. significant at 5% significance level. The results are adjusted for age, sex and educational level of household members, average person in household, religion, caste, place of residence, separate kitchen in household, and state.

their impact on health status in its totality. Therefore, this paper makes an explorative attempt, using a composite index of household environmental standard (HESI), to examine the effect of various household environmental variables on the health outcomes of household population using a national representative sample in India and major states.

This study highlights the fact that a group of population belonging to higher HESI quintile were cherishing healthier life, while the other section of population were experiencing unfavorable health outcomes owing to their relative poorer household environmental status. It is also found that there exist marked inter-state variation in HESI pointing to the fact that, in few states such as Punjab, Gujarat, Haryana and Kerala, household member experience relatively better environmental standards than the states like Bihar, Assam, Orissa and Uttar Pradesh. The prevalence of diseases varies considerably within each HESI quintile according to various background characteristics like place of residence, education, average crowding per room and age of the household members. Interestingly, it has been observed that in spite of high mean HESI score in capital/large city, the disease prevalence is also high. This may be due to large inequality in household environmental conditions in capital/large cities than countryside in India.

Logistic regression also shows that, HESI has statistically significant effect on health outcomes of household members after controlling for other household environmental variables. This implies that the better household environmental condition significantly reduces the risks of contracting infectious diseases. In order to examine the extent of inequality in household environmental standard and its impact upon the individual's health outcomes, concentration cure and concentration index (CI) have been constructed. The concentration curve clearly shows that lesser inequality in the risk of asthma on the one hand, while higher disproportionate concentration of health risks for tuberculosis followed by malaria on the other hand. This is also supported by concentration index indicating greater concentration of vulnerable health outcomes among household members from relatively poorer household environmental standards. Therefore, results from CI support our hypothesis that as one moves from lowest to highest quintile (HESI) the chances of contracting any diseases reduces considerably.

REFERENCES

Audinarayana, N. 2007. Housing environment and child morbidity in rural Andhra Pradesh and Tamil Nadu: An analysis of the NFHS-2 data. In C.P. Prakasam, and R.B., Bhagat, eds., *Population and Environment Linkages.* New Delhi: Rawat Publications.

Broor, S., Pandey, R.M., Ghosh, M., Maitreyi, R.S., Lodha, R., Singal, T., and Kabra, S.K. 2001. Risk factors for severe acute lower respiratory infection in under-give children. *Indian Pediatrics 38*, 1361-1369.

Ezzati, M., and Kammen, D. 2001. Indoor air pollution from biomass combustion and acute respiratory infection in Kenya: An exposure-response study. *Lancet* 358, 619-624.

Gupta, B.N., and Mathur, N. 1997. A study of the household environmental risk factors pertaining to respiratory disease. *Energy and Environment Review* 13, 61-67.

Hazra, A., Dutta, S., and Guha, M. 2007. Effect of household environment on women's health in north-east India. In C.P. Prakasam, and R.B., Bhagat, eds., *Population and Environment Linkages.* New Delhi: Rawat Publications.

International Institute for Population Sciences, and ORC Macro. (2000). National Family Health Survey-2 (NFHS-2), 1998-99: India. Mumbai: International Institute for Population Sciences.

Mishra, V. 2003. Indoor air pollution from biomass combustion and acute respiratory illness in preschool age children in Zimbabwe. *International Journal of Epidemiology* 33, 1-11.

Mishra, V., and Retherford, R.D. 1997. Effects of cooking smoke on prevalence of TB in India. *Population Series Paper No. 92*. October 1997.

Mishra, V., Retherford, R.D., and Smith, K.R. 1999. Biomass cooking fuels and prevalence of tuberculosis in India. *International Journal of Infectious Diseases* 3, 3:119-129.

APPENDIX

Scoring Factors and Summary Statistics for Variables Entering in the Computation of Household Environmental Standard Index, India, NFHS-II, 1998-99

Assets	All India		
	Scoring Factors	Mean	SD
1	2	3	4
Pucca house	0.126	0.348	0.476
Semi-pucca house	-0.031	0.359	0.480
Kachha house	-0.099	0.292	0.455
Own flush toilet	0.120	0.223	0.416
Shared/Public flush toilet	0.040	0.057	0.232
Own pit toilet	0.014	0.144	0.351
Shared/Public pit toilet	0.007	0.025	0.156
No toilet	-0.131	0.550	0.498
Other toilet	-0.003	0.001	0.033
Electricity - source of lighting	0.150	0.667	0.471
Kerosene-source of lighting	-0.149	0.329	0.470
Other source- lighting	-0.007	0.002	0.045

1	2	3	4
Wood-type of fuel	-0.102	0.595	0.491
Dung cakes/crop residues-type of fuel	-0.048	0.097	0.295
Kerosene-type of fuel	0.042	0.072	0.258
LPG-type of fuel	0.124	0.205	0.403
Other fuel	0.020	0.032	0.176
Piped water into residence-source of drinking water	0.119	0.259	0.438
Public tap-source of drinking water	0.003	0.164	0.371
Handpump in residence-source of drinking water	-0.019	0.149	0.356
Public handpump-source of drinking water	-0.063	0.184	0.388
Other source of water	-0.052	0.230	0.421
Seperate kitchen for cooking	0.077	0.570	0.495

Mishra, V., Smith, K.R., and Retherford, R.D. 2005. Effect of cooking smoke and environmental tobacco smoke on acute respiratory infections in young Indian children. *Population and Environment*, 26, 5: 375-396.

Pal, C.1999. *Environmental pollution and development: Environmental pollution policy and judiciary.* New Delhi: Mittal Publications.

Rona, R.J. 1999. Association between asthma and family size between 1977 and 1994. *Journal of Epidemiology and Community Health*, 53, 15-19.

Salmond, C. (1999). Asthma prevalence and deprivation: A small area analysis. *Journal of Epidemiology and Community Health*, 53, 476-480.

World Bank. 2001. Making sustainable commitment: An environmental strategy for the world bank. Accessed online at http://www.worldbank.org

Wu, F., Jacobs, D., Mitchell, C., Miller, D., and Karol, M.H. 2007. Improving indoor environmental air quality for public health: Impediments and policy recommendations. *Environmental Health Perspective*, 115, 6: 953-957.

CHAPTER

Undernourished Children in Shining India

A Call for giving Every Child an Opportunity to Survive

— Sangram Panigrahi

ABSTRACT

Statement of Problem

India is now "shining" as its economic growth has continuously increased with rise in the National income, Percapita income and expenditure. Now we are giving to the importance to rural area by building "Bharat Nirman" from the village through Bottom up approach. Everyone is raising voices for the poor, rural, marginalized, and social excluded people. However, the actual situation is far from the real life. Are we giving importance to the foundation stage of human life? This chapter examines increase in Gross domestic product and per capita income will not automatically improve the development of human life of silent observers i.e. child life. It clearly reflects that increase in economic infrastructure will not automatically benefit to the social status at bottom level.

Methodology and Results

By analyzing the National Family Health Survey Report-3 (2005-06) we found the prevalence of child under nutrition in India is among the highest in the world; nearly double that of Sub-Saharan Africa, with dire consequences for morbidity, mortality, productivity and economic growth. The infant mortality rate in India is 57/1000 live births and the neonatal mortality rate is 39/1000 live births. The stark reality is that almost one in every three babies in the world who die before they are four weeks old is from India. Every year, two million children die in India (UNICEF 2009), accounting for one in five child deaths in the world. It is in India where the entire situation jointly leads to lower Social overhead capital (SOC) i.e. cognitive and school performance, more likely to drop out of school and, as adults are likely to earn lesser incomes that puts pressure on reducing Directive productive activities (DPA) in the economy.

Implications

It needs in coordination and inter Disciplinary approach of different sector to make India signing qualitatively. By implementing policies and programmes is necessary but not sufficient condition to make the "Health as Wealth". While making and implementing the policies, it should take into considerations to what extent and by whom the policies benefit. Besides it, there is also reformulation and design of new ways to solve the problem in sustainable manner.

Introduction

India made progress on the Human Development Index (HDI), i.e. life expectancy to measure longevity, educational attainment to represent knowledge and real gross domestic product (GDP) to represent income where the value that has gone up from 0.595 in 2002 to 0.619 in World Human Development Report (HDR) 2008. On HDI ranking, India has again ranked at 132 of 179 countries. In the gender development index (GDI), India's rank is 116 with .591 points in a universe of 157 countries. On the other India's rank on the Global Hunger index (GHI) is 96th among 119 developing countries. The World Bank report shows declining of the people living below the poverty line of $ 1 a day by 2 percentages reached to 24.3 per cent in three years from 2005-08[1]. It is among the fastest growing economies of the world with substantial growth reported in the industrial and service sectors in the last decade. In spite of the current global economic slowdown, the growth of the Indian economy in 2008-09 is projected at 6 to 6.5 percentage, which would be impressive by global standards as the economies of the developed countries are shrinking. The Economic Survey of 2007-08 (Ministry of Finance, Government of India), has summarised the situation as: The growth of Gross Domestic Product (GDP) at market prices accelerated from 3.8 per cent in 2002-03 to 9.7 per cent in 2006-07, giving an annual growth of 7.9 per cent for the Tenth Five-year Plan. When we come to sector growth in Manufacturing, construction and communications were the leading sectors in the acceleration of growth during the Tenth Five Year Plan, judged by their increased contribution to growth; but share of agriculture in GDP continued, with a decline from 24 per cent in 2001-02 to 17.5 per cent in 2007-08. There is increase in Per capita income growth rate from 2.2 per cent in 2002-03 to 7.2 per cent with Rs. 33,283 in 2007-08. Similarly, per-capita consumption growth rate was up from 1.1 per cent in 2002-03 to 5.3 per cent in 2007-08.

On the other side, instead of the above achievements today. One into three people are still now under the grip of poverty (under whose per capita calorie consumption is less than 2,100 in urban areas and 2,400 in rural areas) – numbers that are often cited as "minimum requirements" in India. The incidence of income poverty has fallen from 36 per cent in the early 1990s to about 25 per cent in 2005. According to the NSSO Report of 2004-05, nearly 20% of the Indian population, about 250 million spent less than Rs 14 per person per day in consumption and 10% percent of rural population spent just Rs 9 per day. In the era of globalized India, 25% of the total population living less than $ 1 per day, which is 16% at the global level and 42 % are living less than $1.25 per day which is 26% at the world level. The situation is very critical in the state like Orissa and Chhattisgarh. In comparison with 30% all India level about 55 to 57 % of rural people in this state found living below the MPCE level of Rs 365 or # 12 a day in 2004-05. Still there are 128 million people having no access to improved drinking water sources and a staggering 665 million defecate in the open. It ultimately leads to negative impact on the health of human capital with special reference to nutritional status of children in India. In this paper, an attempt has made to examine the status of the health of child from the NFHS-3 survey 2005-6 in shining India where government is promising to "inclusive growth" with "Build Bharat" in rural area.

The Problem

Instead of the high economic growth, it is very shameful for us as that India's burgeoning economy has not been kind to the majority of it's children. The disparities between rich and poor are acutely observed in the shocking hunger and malnutrition rates for large numbers of India's children. Nutrition has major effects on health. Nutrition refers to the availability of energy and nutrients to the body's cells in relation to body requirements. Malnutrition refers to any imbalance in satisfying nutrition requirements. Even after decades of efforts and government good intentions, child malnutrition rates in several parts of India are worse than in many sub-Saharan African countries, and they stand out as a paradox in the country. Karin Hulshof, UNICEF India's representative said, "India is home to one fifth of the world's children. Each year one million newborn die during the first month of the life, another million die before they reach first year. Almost 55 million children under 5 years are underweight. Many challenges remain". Of India's one billion plus population of them 158 million are between 0-6 years (TOI 2009). The infant mortality rate in India is 57/1000 live births. The neonatal mortality rate is 39/1000 live births. The stark reality is that almost one in every three babies in the world who die before they are four weeks old is from India. Over half of all women in India are anemic as are 70% of children under the age of five. The issue of underweight children is particularly serious in rural areas and among poorer families, ethnic minorities, lower castes and other socially marginalized groups.

Overview of the Study

The various studies reveals that malnutrition among children is often caused by the synergistic effects of inadequate or improper food intake, repeated episodes of parasitic or other childhood diseases such as diarrhea, and improper care during illness (Pelletier 1994; Ruzicka and Kane 1985). Malnutrition has often cited as an important factor contributing to high morbidity and mortality among children in developing countries (Sommer and Loewenstein 1975; Chen et al. 1980; Vella et al. 1992; Singh 1989; Santhanakrishnan and Ramalingam 1987; Ruzicka and Kane 1985; Serdula 1988; Katz *et al.* 1989; Briend *et al.* 1988). Malnutrition during childhood can also affect growth potential and risk of morbidity and mortality in later years of life. Malnourished children are more likely to grow into malnourished adults who face heightened risks of disease and death. Poor nutritional status of women has been associated with a higher age at menarche (Haq 1984) and a lower age at secondary sterility (Karim *et al.* 1985). A number of factors affect child nutrition, either directly or indirectly. The most commonly cited factors are food availability and dietary intake, breastfeeding, prevalence of infectious and parasitic diseases, access to health care, immunization against major childhood diseases, vitamin A supplementation, maternal care during pregnancy, water supply and sanitation, socioeconomic status, and health-seeking behavior. Demographic characteristics such as the child's age and sex, birth intervals (both preceding and following), and mother's age at childbirth are associated with child nutrition (Sommerfelt 1991). Several studies indicate that inadequate or improper food intake and repeated episodes of infectious diseases adversely affect children's nutritional status (Brown et al. 1982). Lutter and colleagues (1989) found that proper treatment of acute infectious diseases, especially diarrhea, has beneficial effects for children's growth and nutritional status. Briend and colleagues (1988) found that breast-feeding improves nutritional status and child survival. Esrey et al. (1988) and Mertens et al. (1990) found that the presence of a clean water supply and sanitary facilities have beneficial effects on child growth and nutrition.

When I had visited one village of Orissa, I saw health status of the children playing outside is weak. When I asked to their parents are you providing nutritional food to your child. They said it is very difficult to provide two times meal for our child in one day and we simple know food and we are eating for living to struggle for tomorrow. We can imagine that when the parents are not able to arrange the food for two times meal, how they would think about the nutritional food. The arrangement of food for one day is like one year for them. If suppose they aware about the nutritional status then what is the value when they have no capacity to serve this type of food. Their children's sleep with partially fulfilment of their hungry in sunset and awake with searching to fulfil the present hungry and fight with absolute poverty. Their future would continuously fight with poverty as their past and present has passed out in malnutrition. It makes them to join as a child labour for existence. The word like "shining" and "sustainability" is like dreams for them, which would not convert into reality not even in their dreams.

This chapter, does not comment on aiming to double digit of economic growth in India. In fact, we want to know, whether increase in quantitative growth of the economy in terms of income and per-capita reducing the million of baby dies due to lack of proper care and nutrition. This will raise some questions in my mind like: (1) what is the value of theories and policies formulated by the planners of metro city for development of health in rural area? (2) What extent policies and plans have solved the problem? Can it help to meet millennium development goal 2015 or vision 2020? Keeping these questions in base the study has prepared following objectives. The general objective of the study is to give proper importance towards child malnutrition and their future. The specific objectives of the study are:

Objectives

To save the children from the trap of malnutrition death

and suggest some steps for survive them in the childhood stage.

To galvanize much greater political and public engagement with this issue, and much more decisive action by governments and others to help deliver these interventions–not just for some children and their mothers, but for all; and not just in the short term, but through systems and structures that are sustainable.

To effective implementation of the Government policy at the bottom level of the economy for common child affected by this trap

Data and Methodology

The study has included the National Family Health Survey report-3 of 2005-06 for analyzing the health and nutritional status of the children's. The findings of the study on child health have analyses in the following section.

Health of Future Citizen—The Critical Issue

(A) Underweight

Under-nutrition continues to be a major public health problem in India, the most vulnerable groups being women in the reproductive age group and young children. The NFHS fact sheets measured malnutrition, as using three indicators: underweight, stunting, wasting. Firstly, India is home to 40 per cent of the world's malnourished children and 35 per cent of the developing world's low-birth weight infants; (IFPRI 2008), every year two million children die in India (UNICEF 2009), accounting for one in five child deaths in the world. The findings of the National Family Health Survey-3 (NFHS-3) have highlighted the urgent need to turn the spotlight on maternal and child under-nutrition. Indeed, according to the National Family Health Survey (NFHS), the proportion of underweight children remained virtually unchanged between1998-99 and 2005-06 from

43 to 40 per cent for the age group of 0-3 years (See the Fig. 6.1). Nearly 23 per cent of all children born in the country have low birth weight. There is the dead decline in the stunted from 51 to 45% from last 14 year. Under nutrition levels in India remain higher even than for most countries of sub-Saharan Africa, even though those countries are currently much poorer than India, have grown much more slowly, and have much higher levels of infant and child mortality.

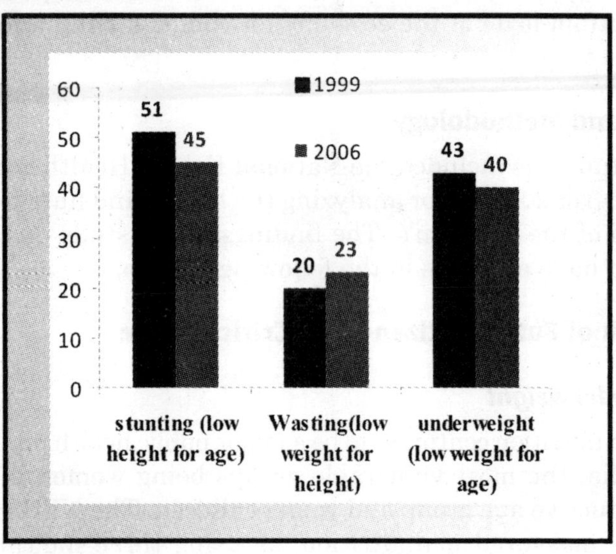

Source: NFHS-3 (2005-6)

Fig. 6.1 : Per cent of children of Underweight 3 Year

(b) Child Mortality

The Table 6.1 presents infant and child mortality rate of India on the reports collected by NFHS-1, 2 and 3. According to these estimates, infant mortality in India has declined from 79 deaths per 1,000 live births in 1991-95 (10-14) years before the survey) to 57 deaths per 1,000 live births in 2001-05 (0-4 years before the survey), thus implying an average rate of decline of 2 infant deaths per 1,000 live births per year. All other measures of infant and child mortality

Table 6.1 : Child Mortality status of NFHS-2, NFHS-2 & NFHS-3 (per 1000 live)

	Average economic growth rate in %	Neo natal mortality	Post Neo natal mortality	Infant mortality	Child mortality	under5 mortality
NFHS-I (1991-95)	5.6	49	30	79	33	109
NFHS-II(1995-99)	5.3	43	24	68	29	95
Change in NFHS I to II*	-0.3	6	6	11	4	14
NFHS-III(1999-2005)	6.6	39	18	57	18	74
Change in NFHS II to III*	1.3	4	6	11	11	21

Source: NFHS-3 (2005-6) *Authors calculation

presented in Table 6.1 also show declining trends during the years before the survey. The neonatal mortality rate has decreased by 10 deaths per 1,000 live births (from 49 to 39), the post neonatal mortality rate has decreased by 12 deaths per 1,000 live births (from 30 to 18), and the child mortality rate (at age 1-4 years) has decreased by 15 deaths per 1,000 children age 1 (from 33 to 18). However, if we examine effect of average economic growth on the child health then the table shows, during the period of NFHS-1(1991-95) the average economic growth is 5.6% and it decline to 5.3% in the period of NFHS-2(1995-99) in India. The decrease in economic growth of 0.3 % impressively reduced the death rate of child significantly. On the other hand, the economic growth has increased from the period of NFHS-2 to NFHS-3 (2000-05) by 1.3% in an average rate. The increase in economic growth has not reduced the problem of child except decline in child mortality and under 5 mortality which reduced by 11 and 21 per 1000 live birth for the period of in comparisons to 4 and 14 per 1000 live birth in the period of NFHS-2. However, in case of neo natal mortality, post neo natal mortality and infant mortality has not reduced positively instead of increase in economic growth of 1.3 in comparisons to the previous period of decline economic growth of 0.3%. Thus from the table it is very clear that the fruit of increase in economic growth has not significantly relate to improve the health status of children In spite of these impressive declines, one out of every 14 children born during the five years before NFHS-3 will die before reaching age five.

Neonatal mortality: The probability of dying in the first month of life.

Post neonatal mortality: The probability of dying after the first month of life but before the first birthday.

Infant mortality (1q0): The probability of dying before the first birthday.

Child mortality (4q1): The probability of dying between the first and fifth birthdays.

Under-five mortality (5q0): The probability of dying before the fifth birthday.

Figure 6.2 shows that during the period of 1991-95 and 1995-99 the average annual economic growth rate fall in 0.3% that has reduced neonatal and post neo natal mortality by 6, infant mortality by 11, child mortality 4 and under 5 mortality 14 per 1000 live birth. On the other in the period of change in 1999-2005, the average annual economic growth rate increase by 1.3 per cent, which has reduced neonatal mortality by 4, post neo natal mortality by 11 and infant mortality by 11 per 1000 live birth. There is dead decline of neo natal, post neonatal and infant mortality rate instead of positive economic growth It clearly indicates that there is no direct relation between quantitative economic growth and health status of the child. On the other hand, the increase in economic growth of 1.3 per cent has significantly decline child mortality by 11 and under 5 yrs mortality by 21 per 1000 live birth in India. However, in the case of underweight, Neo natal mortality and infant mortality has not change significantly by increase in annual economic growth rate. It clearly shows to what extent we are giving importance to make our child health as wealth of the future.

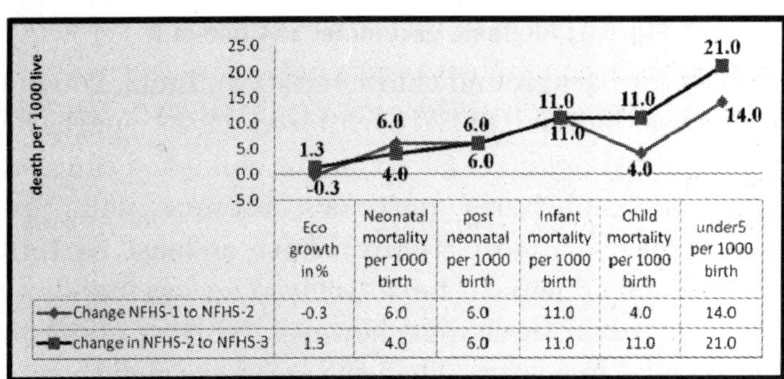

	Eco growth in%	Neonatal mortality per 1000 birth	post neonatal per 1000 birth	Infant mortality per 1000 birth	Child mortality per 1000 birth	under5 per 1000 birth
Change NFHS-1 to NFHS-2	-0.3	6.0	6.0	11.0	4.0	14.0
change in NFHS-2 to NFHS-3	1.3	4.0	6.0	11.0	11.0	21.0

Fig. 6.2 : Economic Growth VS Child health Status

(c) Child Immunization

Figure 6.3 shows the Percentage of children age 12-23 months who received specific vaccines (BCG, measles, and three doses each of DPT and polio vaccine) at any time before

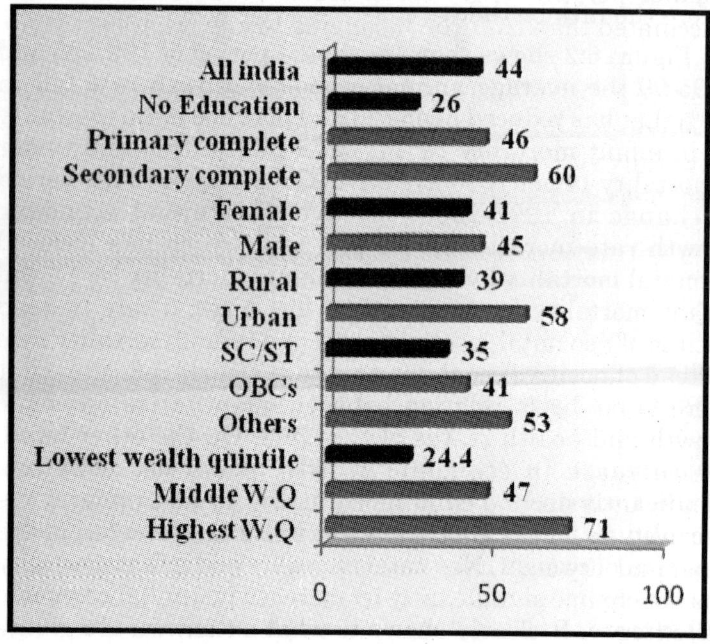

Source: NFHS-3 (2005-6)

Fig. 6.3 : All Basic Vaccinated to Child in %

the survey (by background characteristics), India, 2005-06. In India Less than half (44%) of children, 12-23 months has fully vaccinated against the six major childhood illnesses: tuberculosis, diphtheria, pertussis, tetanus, polio, and measles. However, most children have at least partially vaccinated, only 5 percent have received no vaccinations at all. There is very little change, however, NFHS-2 (42%) and NFHS- 3 (44%) in 5 years. The boys (45%) are slightly more likely in comparisons to girls (42%) has fully vaccinated. On the other 58% of children in urban areas age 12-23 months have received all of the recommended vaccinations by the time of the survey, compared with only 39% of children in rural areas. The Vaccination coverage for each type of vaccine is much higher in urban areas than in rural areas. A much smaller percentage of SC/STs children (35 percent) has fully vaccinated than children belonging to any other caste/tribe status. As expected, household wealth index has a strong positive relation with vaccination coverage. Only 24 per cent of children from households in the lowest wealth quintile have fully vaccinated, compared with 71 per cent of children from households in the highest wealth quintile. Only 26 per cent of children of mothers with no education has fully vaccinated while 46 per cent of children of mothers who have completed primary and 60 per cent for secondary has fully vaccinated, and the percentage vaccinated rises steadily with increasing levels of education. Progress in vaccination coverage varies widely among the states. Less than one-third of children has fully vaccinated in Nagaland, Uttar Pradesh, Rajasthan, Arunachal Pradesh, and Assam. At the other end of the spectrum, at least three-quarters of children have received all the recommended vaccinations in Tamil Nadu, Goa, and Kerala.

(D) Integrated Child Development (ICD) Service

The ICDS programme provides nutrition and health services for children under age 6 years and (2005-6) pregnant or breastfeeding women, as well as preschool activities for

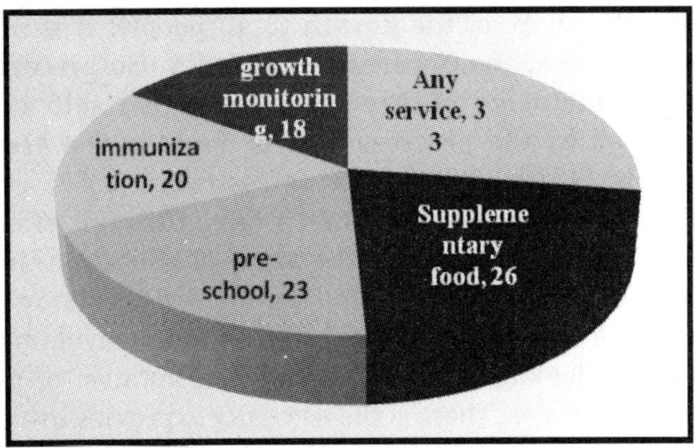

Fig. 6.4 : ICDS Service in % (NFHS-3)

children age 3 to 6 years. This service is providing through community-based anganwadi centers. The reports shows that 81% of children under six who are in areas covered by an anganwadi centre, one-third 33% receive services of some kind from the centre (Fig. 6.4). The most common services children receive are supplementary food (26% of children under 6) and preschool (23% of children age 3-6). One-fifth of children receive vaccinations and growth monitoring services at the anganwadi centre.

Measures within Challenge

On the above backdrop we can say that increase in economic growth is always welcome but with qualitative way by improving health status of the human resources. There is the urgent requirement of ways to solve the problem by sustainable development of the child with women. Following are some steps to solve the problem of health with special reference to child in India.

(1) Inclusive growth with sustainability

The first step to solve the problem is to give importance to the economic growth in inclusive manner. It simply refers to provide the share of the growth to all people. It is indeed noteworthy that the Government of India (GoI) recognises that the 'inclusive nature of the growth itself will be conditioned by the progress that is made in the areas of education, health and physical infrastructure. The goal of inclusive growth can be achieve only through effective government intervention in the areas of education, health and support to the needy. Value for every tax rupee spent to be ensuring by emphasizing the outcomes and avoiding any wastage or leakages in the delivery mechanism of public goods and services. There is the necessity to provide livelihood with sustainability which help them to more cautious about the own health with also their child.

(2) Programme at bottom-up

The developing countries need to implement national plans for reducing maternal, newborn and child mortality. Some of these plans exist on paper, but has not implemented effectively. There is the need to improve the programme and its implementation from bottom up level. In other words, plans will need to be developed or significantly strengthened from ground level. The plan should sit within a coherent development strategy for the country, and be properly integrated with action to tackle intermediate and underlying causes of maternal, newborn and child mortality. An important lesson that we can draw from the NGO community is that it is important to identify local partners, be it the administration (District Collector, CDPO, CMHO or even a block level supervisor or local leaders and groups, including the Panchayat in rural area.

(3) Train and deploy more health workers

Every country should have a credible plan for reducing maternal, newborn and child mortality. This should focus on scaling up proven interventions like effective antenatal care, skilled attendance at birth, early postnatal care, vitamin A supplementation, community case management of diarrhea, pneumonia and malaria, and increased access to immunization and vaccines. As part of the effort to increase access to basic health services, donors, international institutions and developing countries need to recruit, train, equip and deploy many more health workers. There is the necessity of quantitative appointment of health workers and increase in quality of the service provided by them to the needy people. Besides it, education and employment to the women, Awareness by media and welfare scheme for child also helps to solve the problem in consistent manner.

In order to reduce malnutrition, one must understand its causes. Thus, we should give importance to three household-level underlying determinants: food security, adequate care for mothers and children, and a proper health environment. Finally, the underlying determinants has influenced by the basic determinants: the potential resources available to a country or community, and a host of political, cultural, and social factors that affect their utilization. The study focuses on the underlying determinants, using four variables to represent them: national food availability (for food security), women's education and women's status relative to men's (for the quality of care), and access to safe water (for the quality of the health environment). Finally, under and unemployment, low wages, gender disparities, unfair trade practices, drought and lack of information supported by strong political will must be tackled simultaneously to ensure sustainable results. This will certainly take much longer, but not addressing these issues can only mean cosmetic solutions

Conclusion

It is disconcerting to observe our concentration is to raise the economic growth in quantitatively by making the plans, fixing the targets to make the country developed. If we want to achieve it then we should move qualitatively with the help of education, health and standard of living of the downturn people in the economy. The alarming proportions of under-nutrition and its heavy concentration among the poor irrefutably consign India to being one of the unconvincing performers in child health. Undoubtedly, from a policy perspective, more attention needs to focus on improving child health conditions in to make their future signing. Given the state of affairs, the government both central and State should work towards enhancing the effectiveness of the existing schemes or should engineer new mechanisms to resolve the problems. Only implementation of the programmes and schemes is not a necessary condition but the impact of the programmes to the common people and proper account of the expenditure is sufficient ways make India shining qualitatively. The unsystematic implementation and poor performance of the Integrated Child Development Scheme (ICDS) has not offered much to celebrate (Das Gupta *et al.* 2006), nonetheless with effective design, community-based approach and wider coverage of ICDS along with the newly launched National Rural Health Mission (NRHM) of India can help to make improvement in the health status of children. It would be more encouraging if interventions of health design based on regular and systematic assessment.

REFERENCES

General studies Indian Economy *'Pratiyogita Darpan extra issue',* Upkar Prakashan 2009-10

Briend, A., B. Wojtyniak, and M. G. M. Rowland (1988): "Breast feeding, nutritional status, and child survival in rural Bangladesh" *British Medical Journal,* 296(6626): 879–82.

Brown, K. E., R. E. Black, and S. Becker (1982): "Seasonal changes in nutritional status and the prevalence of malnutrition in a longitudinal study of young children in rural Bangladesh" *American Journal of Clinical Nutrition* 36(2): 303–13.

Chen, L. C., A. K. M. A. Chowdhury, and S. L. Huffman (1980): "Anthropometric assessment of energy-protein malnutrition and subsequent risk of mortality among preschool aged children" *American Journal of Clinical Nutrition* 33(8): 1836–45.

Das gupta. M, Gragnolati, M., Bredenkamp, Lee. Y, Sekhar, M (2006): " ICDS and Persistent Under nutrition Strategies to Enhance the Impact", *Economic and political weekly,* March 25

Esrey, S. A., J. P. Habicht, and M. C. Latham (1988): "Drinking water source, diarrheal morbidity, and child growth in villages with both traditional and improved water supplies in rural Lesotho, Southern Africa" *American Journal of Public Health* 78(11): 1451–55.

Haq, M. N. (1984): "Age at menarche and the related issue: A pilot study on urban school girls" *Journal of Youth and Adolescence* 13(6): 559–67.

International Food Policy Research Institute, Accelerating Progress toward Reducing Child Malnutrition in India,A Concept for Action, IFPRI, Washington, 2008.

Katz, J., K. P. West, Jr., I. Tarwotjo, and A. Sommer (1989): "The importance of age in evaluating anthropometric indices for predicting mortality" *American Journal of Epidemiology* 130(6): 1219–26.

Karim, A., A. K. M. A. Chowdhury, and M. Kabir (1985): "Nutritional status and age at secondary sterility in rural Bangladesh" *Journal of Biosocial Science* 17(4): 497–502.

Lutter, C. K., J. O. Mora, J. P. Habicht., K. M. Rasmussen, D. S. Robson, S. G. Sellers, C.M. Super, and M. G. Herrera (1989): "Nutritional supplementation: Effects on child stunting because of diarrhoea" *American Journal of Clinical Nutrition* 50(1): 1–8.

Mertens, T. E., M. A. Fernando, S. N. Cousens, B. R. Kirkwood, T. F. Marshall, and R. G. Feachem (1990): "Childhood diarrhoea in Sri Lanka: A case-control study of the impact of improved water sources" *Tropical Medicine and Parasitology* 41(1): 98–104.

National Health Family Survey Reports-3 (2006): "International Institute of population sciences" Mumbai.

National Sample Survey Organisation (2004): "Report of Ministry of statistics and programme Implementation" *www.mospi.gov.in/mospi_**nsso**_rept_pubn.ht*

Pelletier, D. L. (1994): "The relationship between child anthropometry and mortality in developing countries: Implications for policy, programs and future research" *Journal of Nutrition Supplement* 124(10S): 2047S–2081S.

Ruzicka, L. T. and P. Kane (1985): "Nutrition and child survival in south Asia. In K. Srinivasan and S. Mukerji, eds. *Dynamics of population and family welfare*, pp. 333–57. Bombay: Himalaya Publishing House.

Santhanakrishnan, B. R. and R. Ramalingam (1987): "Risk factors of mortality in children with diarrhoeal disease in Madras", *India. Journal of Diarrhoeal Disease Research* 5(1): 36–9.

Singh, K. P (1989): "Green revolution and child survival in the state of Punjab" In *International Population Conference, New Delhi: Proceedings*, Vol. 1, pp. 379–88. Liege, Belgium: International Union for the Scientific Study of Population (IUSSP).

Serdula, M. (1988): "Diet, malnutrition in Sub-Saharan Africa: Abstract. *Annales de l'IFORD* 12(2): 35–63.

Sommer, A. and M. S. Loewenstein (1975): "Nutritional status and mortality: A prospective validation of the QUAC stick" *American Journal of Clinical Nutrition* 28(3): 287–92

Sommerfelt, A. E. and M. K. Stewart (1994): "*Children's nutritional status*" DHS Comparative Studies, No. 12. Calverton, Maryland: Macro International, Demographic and Health Surveys (DHS).

Sommerfelt, A. E. (1991): “Comparative analysis of the determinants of children’s nutritional status” In *Demographic and Health Surveys World Conference: Proceedings*, Vol. 2, pp. 981–98. Columbia, Maryland: Institute for Resource Development/Macro International, Demographic and Health Surveys (DHS).

Vella, V., A. Tomkins, A. Borghesi, G. B. Migliori, B. C. Adriko, and E. Crevatin (1992a) “Determinants of child nutrition and mortality in north-west Uganda” *Bulletin of the World Health Organization* 70(5): 637–43.

Times of India (2009) “India has the largest number of stunted children: UNICEF” 14-Nov-2009

UNICEF (2009): “State of the World’s Children” p. 119.

CHAPTER

Right to Accessibility of Health Care

An Oasis for HIV/AIDS Patients

— Skylab Sahu

Introduction

Of late, right to health has been considered by the apex court as an extended part of the 'right to life' under Article 21 of the Indian Constitution. As per the directives of the Supreme Court, therefore, the right to health is a part of fundamental rights. The health right makes the state obliged to respect, protect1 and fulfil certain factors, which, in turn, can ensure right to health to all (ICESCR, Article 12 PART II). Thus, the state while respecting right to health has to stand by the measures of the rights such as accessibility, availability, and acceptability (Marks and Stephen 2004). The state has to ensure that under accessibility, no citizen is denied of health care and services because of any means: physical distance, and economic constraints. In addition, accessibility without discrimination is one of the major considerations that have to be ensured by the State. Even when a person has some health problems associated with social stigma and discrimination like HIV/AIDS, she/he required to be provided with accessibility of health care without discrimination. HIV/AIDS has been declared a national health problem and several Indian States (high and low HIV prevalence States) have taken numerous measures in terms of policy, and strategies to combat the epidemic. Even though the high prevalence state like Karnataka and a low prevalence State like West Bengal follow the Central Government's approach, have been performing differently in taking many initiatives that could lead to difference in ensuring right to health to HIV patients.[1]

In this chapter, we have considered only one parameter of health rights, i.e. the right to accessibility of health care and treatment. We initially discussed the meaning of accessibility of health care and outlined the indicators for accessibility with special reference to HIV as a health issue. We then analysed whether people living with HIV/AIDS are guaranteed with the accessibility of health care and treatment. This follows identification and examination of factors responsible for violation of rights to accessibility for HIV positive people or HIV patients. Finally, we have analysed measures to curtail violation of right to accessibility towards ensuring health rights to HIV positive people. Although HIV/AIDS is a national health problem, we had discussed whether accessibility of health care varies in two different States, i.e. Karnataka and West Bengal. The section below provides a brief overview of the methodology of the study.

Methodology

This study is based on both secondary as well as primary data collection and analysis. We have selected two States, i.e. Karnataka (as one the high HIV prevalence States) and West Bengal (as one of the low HIV prevalence States). In contrast, West Bengal is one of the most vulnerable towards highest occurrence State for HIV/AIDS. The detection of the HIV cases made by Anti-natal Care centres shows that West Bengal state has 0.84 percentages of HIV prevalence rate. The estimation made by ANC (anti-natal care centres) projected one per cent of the incidence rate for Karnataka.

In absolute numbers[2] in Karnataka as well as in West Bengal, there were 39,491 and 6,941 HIV positive people respectively (the data are included till 31st January 2006) (Indiastat 2009). These two States also differ in case of availability of health care facilities in terms of health care centres, doctors and so on. We analyse whether with the difference of availability of facilities whether accessibility of health care by HIV positive also differs.

In order to portray the field reality, we have taken help of interviews, observation, and case studies. For secondary literature, we have depended on existing literature, news clippings and so on. To understand the role of the State, we relied on NACO's guideline on AIDS, statement of State AIDS Cell Societies etc. Primary data are collected through interview and group discussion method in order to obtain information from government officers, individual activists, NGO activists, and doctors in hospitals who are attending to AIDS patients.

Since it is extremely difficult to interview HIV positive men or women within the family, due to inherent privacy of it, we have drawn our samples from institutions[3]. We initially collected the list of hospitals i.e, public, private and NGO led-hospitals where treatment to HIV positive people is provided. Through lottery method, we selected three government hospitals having VCTCT, PPTCT or ART centres within it. Similarly, we made a list of civil society organisation led (Civil society organisation) hospitals, from which, we selected two hospitals each. However, we had decided to include private hospitals, but could not get permission from most private hospitals to collect information or to draw samples.

As our emphasis was on women's health, we obtained the list of HIV affected female patients who visited hospitals for treatment and after getting the list, a random sampling was done to draw hundred[4] each women from the states. In addition, we have also taken a few case studies of HIV positive male members to understand the male perspective on the issue.

The Right to Accessibility of Health Care: Meaning

Human rights constitute some entitlements to guarantee rights to individuals. The responsibility of the state lies in protecting, promoting, respecting and fulfilling the entitlements. The State must not ever violate the human rights standard, and the state authorities must not come in the way of people from educating themselves (Cheria *et al.*, 2004). For instance, in a medical set up, a patient has every right to ask about her/his illness and the medicine for treatment, possible repercussions of the treatment on the patient and also can ask about the side-effects of any disease. This aspect of the State obligation coincides with the right to information. The States need to prevent the third parties from destroying the quality of life. The third parties are the private agencies, those who are involved in health care or health services. Moreover, the State has to take several measures to ensure accessibility of health care. In the process, the State should formulate policies, make financial allocations and ensure proper implementation of the policies or programmes such that the above-mentioned criteria can be fulfilled.

Accessibility of health care also includes provisioning of health care in such a way that no person would face any difficulty in terms of health care accessibility. In such case a person is likely to access health care within the government medical set up irrespective of any difficulties, in terms of geographical location, financial position and any such constraints. Right to accessibility includes accessibility of information relating diseases, cure of diseases and prevention from the diseases. It also means adequate availability of counselling to HIV positive people that provides psychological healing to them. It means provisioning of treatment of patients without denial of treatment, without discrimination, and treatment with consent. In total, we have addressed accessibility through four measures i.e., treatment without discrimination and denial, treatment without geographical and economic constraints, right to information, and adequate and proper counselling.

Treatment without Discrimination and Denial

Treatment without discrimination is a major part of right to accessibility of health care. Treatment denial directly violates right to accessibility of health care of people. Instances are reported every day, doctors denying medical treatment to people tested HIV positive[5], and often doctors conduct HIV test - even without their knowledge. In the selected states, I have come across several cases where HIV positive people have faced discrimination and treatment denial. Incidences of discriminations were found both in private as well as public hospitals. We found cases where people were not permitted for admission and for treatment in a few private hospitals because of their HIV positive status. In many government hospitals, too para-medical staff often have discriminated HIV positive patients, and in a few cases even doctors have been found to mistreat HIV/AIDS patients. Unfortunately, most such rights violation cases have remained unnoticed by the State governments. As can be seen from Table 7.1, in West Bengal hospitals, more number of discrimination cases (respondents faced discrimination) has taken place than in Karnataka hospitals. In Karnataka, the number of patients who faced discrimination in government hospitals is lower (41.66) than in West Bengal (73.52) based government hospitals. However, discrimination rate is higher in private hospitals in Karnataka (58.33) than in West Bengal (26.47). There are cases of treatment denial and discrimination in both the states. In all the hospitals, doctors do hesitate to carry out surgery on HIV positive patients. Recently, in Karnataka, a HIV positive woman (who was our respondent) was forced to deliver her baby without the doctor's support but the incidence went unreported. From our field work, we came to know that in a few government hospitals (like Calcutta Medical College and North Bengal Medical College) of West Bengal, in-house patients are instructed to post a sticker on their forehead indicating the diseases they suffer from. As some HIV positive male and female patients mentioned, they had to put a sticker as HIV positive, which in turn, invited stigma and discrimination.

Table 7.1 : Number of Respondents who Faced Discrimination in Different Hospitals (West Bengal and Karnataka)

Discrimination in Different Hospitals	West Bengal	Karnataka
Discrimination faced in Government hospitals	25	10
Discrimination Faced in Private hospitals	9	14
Never faced discrimination in any hospital	76	86
Total	**100**	**100**

Source: Primary Data

In Karnataka, the incidence of discrimination persists, although relatively less number of respondents reported to have faced discrimination and ill-treatment. In one of the cases in Bowring hospital (specialised hospital for HIV/AIDS treatment) of Karnataka, Sultana (name changed) an HIV positive woman, faced trouble in accessing health care. A 27-years old, Sultana reported certain disquieting facts about the hospital: The ART centre in Bowring Hospital does not have a lady doctor and the only doctor who does check up for patient is a virology specialist. Thus, any woman who comes with gynaecology problems is referred to the gynaecologist of the hospital. During the interview Sultana[6] complained about her own illness i.e. consistent and continuing problem of white-discharge. When we asked whether the doctor had done a medical check up, she mentioned that she had stopped going to the gynaecologists as she had been ill-treated thrice by the lady doctor with foul words, '*pata nahin kahan kahan se aajate hain, jab dekho* (she used foul word ——) *dikhane ke liye taiyar rahte hain, pata nahin kya kya karte hain aur kya kya bimari leke chale aate hain, hamara jaan khatain hain*'. (No body knows where from these people come, every time remains ready for showing——, and god knows to which profession they are into (suspected to be sex workers). She said that the doctor had abused her and did not even attend her properly, and hence she was no more interested in going to the doctor. Rather, she felt it was better to bear the infection and pain than being abused by the lady doctor in the public hospital. As Sultana is a poor woman, it was very difficult for her to go to a private gynaecologist. Sultana's plight is not an isolated one; such inhuman acts brings to the fore the paramount need to sensitising the medical profession to the need for upholding medical ethics in dealing with poor patients particularly in the context of ensuring health rights.

We found certain curious incidences, i.e., some HIV positive people (both men and women) not revealing their HIV positive status before the doctors and yet receiving treatment for HIV. In such cases, there is possibility that HIV positive people even knowing their seropositive status may not reveal it before any doctor unless it is really necessary. During my field work I came across Bhimsen (name changed), a HIV positive person, and works in a care unit meant for HIV/AIDS in West Bengal. Once he faced a minor accident and got an injury. He was in immediate need of the first aid and some minor treatment. He went to the nearby doctor and was treated without disclosing his HIV status. His claim was that if he had revealed his HIV status, the doctor would not have done the first-aid treatment for him. Bhimsen being associated with an HIV care unit for 7 months knows the possible repercussion to hide his health status before the doctor who treated him without using 'universal precautionary measures'[7]. In such a case, Bhimsen may be alleged following unethical practice or attitude because of hiding his health status before the doctor. The doctor was very susceptible to infection. When we questioned him on ethical grounds, Bhimsen said he is not repenting for his act, and on the contrary he asked us (which put all of us in a dilemma) 'what is ethics? Whether ethics is greater than life? Such a straightforward statement from Bhimsen was very astonishing. He said further 'when doctors don't treat us, and it is their duty to treat patients still they refuse treatment, and then is it not unethical from their side'? From this case study it is also inferred that accessibility to health care has not been guaranteed to all patients.

The questions posed by Bhimsen and the approach observed by him also can be followed by any one, who because of the fear of denial could keep his seropositive status secret before the doctors. Such cases in turn can make doctors vulnerable to infection. Therefore, there is a need for the doctors to retrospect their attitude to HIV positive people and take necessary steps accordingly.

Treatment without Geographic and Economic Constraints

As far as HIV/AIDS is concerned, the Indian Central Government has taken several steps towards provisioning of health care for HIV positive people. It has established several centres like Voluntary Counselling and Testing Centres (VCTC), Prevention of Mother to Child Transmission (PMTCT), and Anti Retro Viral Therapy centres (ART), care centres and so on. At State level, governments are implementing policies and programmes led by central government. However, the implementation of all policies has not been uniformly done by all the States. Therefore, based on the differences of availability of health facilities HIV positive people face different experience of accessibility of health care. There is different performance of Karnataka and West Bengal States that in turn, affects HIV positive people differently in two States. In the state of West Bengal, for instance, people face in-accessibility due to geographical reasons as the VCTC centres are set up at the district level. As a result, people residing at suburb areas find it difficult to reach to the district head quarter. Moreover, when most of the district hospitals instead of treating HIV patients refer HIV cases to another district hospital (Kolkata) then if becomes further problematic for people to access health care, as distance may appear as a hurdle for many people. Constraints due to geographical distance are also added up with the economic constraints (as additional travel charge may be difficult to bear) that prevent in availing health care facilities. In Karnataka, however the VCTC centres are established at the block level that makes it little more convenient for HIV positive people to approach health care centres than in West Bengal. Therefore, it is quite clear that more number of health centres in West Bengal are urban based whereas, in Karnataka, as centres are also located at semi urban and rural areas. When ART centres are not set up adequately and it is established at a central place, a majority of the HIV positive people being economically powerless fail to afford ART from the near by private medicine shop and also face difficulty in travelling a long distance. When they either fail to travel or fail to afford the ART medicine (costs one thousand rupees per month) die with the diseases. In West Bengal while there is only one ART centre located in Kolkata district (Table 7.2), in Karnataka there are four centres. Inadequate availability and improper allocation of centres and medicine and improperly managed health care centres violates right to accessibility.

Table 7.2: Infrastructure Created by the States under National AIDS Control Programme

(As on to December 2005) (In numbers)

India	Sentinel Surveillance Sites	VCTC Centres	ART Centres	PPTCT Centres	STD Centres	Blood Banks Modernised	Targeted Intervention Centres/ Project	Community Care centres	Drop-in Centres
West Bengal	35	27	1	10	37	82	45	3	7
Karnataka	66	123	4	59	41	78	37	12	1
All India	**750**	**1,114**	**57**	**485**	**829**	**1,179**	**908**	**85**	**70**

Source: Indiastat 2009

In an interview, Ferjana, the vice president of West Bengal Network of Positive people (WBNP+) mentioned that because of acute poverty many rural based HIV positive people find it difficult to come to Kolkata every month to get the ART drugs. Most of the time distance and economic constraints act as hurdles for people to access health care. In Karnataka, for some people coming to Bangalore-based hospital is a choice, as the city has anonymity, many of them in order to hide their health status prefer to come to Bangalore. However, for a few, travelling from far off suburb districts and spending 6 to 7 hours on travelling to reach hospital is highly inconvenient. In contrast, in W.B. visiting Kolkata for treatment for almost all respondents was a necessity and not choice. Only two women visited the Kolkata based hospital for the sake of anonymity[8]. Most of the women coming from far off places felt it inconvenient to come to Kolkata every month.

Particularly in suburb and rural areas many people die because they fail to access health care. Even during my field study I found similar findings where poor and people coming from far off districts revealed that it is extremely difficult for them to travel every month a long distance and to reach Kolkata for the medicine. It takes a whole day and sometimes more than a day, in an unknown city, everything costs money, food and staying and so on. Many of them reiterated that it is difficult to access health care. The following section focuses how improper information flow also can lead to inaccessibility of health care.

Right to Information

A patient has right to know the disease he/she has, medicines he or she is taking and its function as well as the side effects of the medicine. However, in most of the cases medical personal do not explain all necessary facts to patients. In some cases a few doctors have not felt it necessary to reveal the patient about their own sickness. In a few case, it can prove fatal. For instance, in case of HIV/AIDS if a doctor doesn't reveal the patient about her or his HIV positive status, it may be fatal not only for the patient but also for others. A case study shows such an incidence.

CASE STUDY–I

Mamta, a 27-year old widow, is working as a digital operator in a Bangalore based private company, geting Rs. 4,000 per month. She has a 7-year old daughter. Since four years, after her husband's death, she has been staying with her mother and sister. During the first fifteen minutes of the discussion with her I found her to be strong and courageous. At that moment I noticed that her desires, ambition was not different from any other normal woman. For instance, like a normal woman she wished to see her daughter healthy, good in studies and sports. But, despite all the ambitions, she never forgot the reality of her health status. All her worries and tension were expressed in the later part of her interview. She said her daughter used to be very active in studies and sports, but for the past four to five months, she has not been able to concentrate on her studies and sports. Since Mamta is in the symptomatic stage (that is beginning of AIDS), she is getting one or the other problem. While explaining the way through which a drastic change occurred in her life, she referred to her marriage and her life with her husband. She got married at the age of 19 to a government civil engineer who was then 35 years old. She found her husband to be very cooperative. She spent around two years happily with him. However, during the first year of her married life, her husband used to have regular health complications like cold and fever. She was not worried much for such minor fever and cold as her husband also used to consult a doctor (a particular doctor of a private clinic in Vijayanagar, Bangalore) and used to assure her that he was not having any serious health problem. After one year, she also started suffering from problems like fever, dysentery, cold and cough. She said she didn't have any major diseases prior to her marriage, so she hardly visited any hospital particularly before her marriage. Her husband took her to the same doctor where her husband used to visit for treatment. During her first visit to the clinic, she was asked to do a blood test. However, neither her husband nor the doctor revealed the result of the test except for saying 'nothing to be worried about'. In spite of regular problems and treatment, nothing much improved in her health condition. Just after the second year of her marriage she also became pregnant. She delivered her baby without knowing that she is HIV positive. Her husband neither disclosed that both of them were HIV positive nor did he restrict her to deliver a baby who later on also became HIV positive. Her husband subsequently became more sick and died after three years of her daughter's birth. Her husband never disclosed his HIV status to her. She went to the doctor and asked about the history of her husband's illness as well as her own illness. She was shocked to know that her husband died of HIV and she was also having HIV. It was more astonishing for her when she knew that her husband was HIV infected even before their marriage. Thus, the doctor kept this fact, a secret, due to which Mamta and her little daughter are suffering now. The case study brings to the fore several ethical issues and provides a new dimension to women's vulnerability to HIV, beyond already existing stereotypical susceptibility of women. Mamta's husband concealed his HIV status and got married to her, infected her and without disclosing his HIV positive status got an infected child. Moreover, the doctor kept everything secret from Mamta, which is unethical from the doctor's side. Here, both her husband and the doctor were not only unethical but had also violated Mamta's human rights. Her husband pretended to be cooperative, faithful and caring, but in reality, he didn't mind infecting his wife and child. The case study also draws attention towards the debate on the issue of universal mandatory blood testing on HIV for both male and female before marriage.

In such a situation where a doctor was also responsible for the infection of Mamta and her kid the question is what should be the role of the doctor. At least in the above case when Mamta visited the doctor for the first time the doctor could have told her and if not at least after Mamta got infected with HIV then the doctor could have revealed her about her infection. In the process two lives i.e. of Mamta and her daughter could have been saved by the doctor.

In another case, a woman Sumi (name changed) an SC woman who was treated along with her son in a private hospital of West Bengal, were given ART without CD4 check up by the doctor, even without the knowledge of the respondent. When the respondent became bankrupt often paying for private treatment, thereafter, because of her dilapidated economic condition, she was forced to go to the government hospital. In the government hospital, she got the information that before starting ART, a mandatory test of CD4 was most essential. Such issues focus on the violation of right to accessibility of information and also points out the need for the regulation of private hospitals. In this background, information and counselling may work as effective tools in preventing people from the infection and treating people psychologically as well.

Adequate and Proper Counselling

Counselling to people in general and to HIV positive people in particular is necessary ways of ensuring right to accessibility. Adequate counselling makes people aware regarding the illness, cure and prevention. In the process the general public remain aware regarding HIV and may in the process take measures to avoid the diseases. Counselling to HIV positive people helps a person more effectively than just giving medicine to her/him. Counselling builds psychological strength which makes HIV positive people to live life enthusiastically even after the infection. In the selected states, there are many cases where people have been taking ART since 7/8 years and are still fit and have eagerness to live like a normal person. Besides, some government hospital doctors and counsellors have positively changed their family members' attitude towards HIV positive person(s) through counselling.

Counselling has been considered as a mandatory procedure as it functions as a vital preventive strategy for providing awareness and information; counselling also acts as a check to human rights violation, likely to take place in the process of HIV test. Four kinds of counselling are recommended relating to HIV issue, given in different situations. These are pre-test counselling, post test counselling, Pre-ART counselling and Post ART or follow up counselling. The pre-test counselling is most important for all people (even for people who are not HIV positive) whose consent is required for HIV test. Post-test counselling protects a person from a major breakdown in case that person is found HIV positive after the test.

From our study it was found that there has not been adequate provisioning of counselling by the centres. In the process, many people have been devoid of health information. Inadequate counselling may create socio-psychological problems that in turn may affect a person's physical health adversely. In Karnataka, in most of the Voluntary Counselling and Testing Centres (VCTCT), or even Prevention of Mother to Child Transmission (PMTCT) centres, government hospitals or even at any blood bank, consent before HIV test is not taken from individuals. Only after the disclosure of the HIV positive status of people, they are provided with the post-test counselling. There are hardly a few government hospitals that provide pre-test counselling. Even the most reputed hospitals, that are supposed to have integrated facilities and services, do not provide pre-test counselling to people, whereas in a few government hospitals having VCTCT/PMTCT centres in West Bengal, people are provided with pre-test counselling. In the private hospitals or blood banks of both the states, the situation is still worse where neither pre-test counselling, nor post-test counselling is given to HIV positive people. These are clear cases of violation of human rights in hospitals which have failed to impart awareness or information and psychological support to people in general and HIV positive people in particular.

As we found, in a large number of cases people have been facing difficulties in accessing health care. In both the states when people faced discrimination, in West Bengal people faced more trouble in accessing health care due to improper establishment of health centres and in adequate number of health centres. In both the state there were instances of treatment denial. Moreover, it was also found that HIV positive people faced plight in a few private hospitals as well. The information relating diseases and treatment did not flow well to the patient and in all such case HIV positive people's rights remained under threat of violation. In this situation question arises why any HIV positive person face medical paranoia. The following section explains the answer.

Dealing with Medical Paranoia and Steps to Ensure Accessibility

The HIV positive people face social stigma and discrimination due to several reasons and one of the main reasons is because of the fear that is inherent among people regarding the illness. As far as HIV/AIDS is concerned, as mentioned above a large chunk of medical staff also stigmatise and discriminate HIV positive people. Behind such actions of the medical staff there may be fear of infection ingrained. In most of the cases doctors show their apathy towards carrying out surgery to HIV positive people. During the field work I met several HIV positive people and doctors who mentioned this fact. Apart from surgery, even there are many doctors who do not treat a patients' simple illness if that person is HIV positive. Even we found this fact from the above mentioned case study of Bhimsen. In the process, the medical staff assume that all other people either who do not reveal their HIV positive status or people who have not gone for HIV test are not HIV positive. Irrespective of their assumptions doctors generally do not take universal percussion measures that can prevent doctor from the infection knowingly and unknowingly.

It is astonishing that even twenty years after the discovery of the virus, attitude of most of the doctors has remained unchanged. Despite conducting specific trainings programmes, seminars and workshops to sensitise the doctors, there appears to be hardly any change in the attitude of most doctors, towards HIV positive patients. Though HIV/ AIDS has been made part of the medical science curriculum a large number of doctors have still not shed their fear of HIV infection.

In such case, question occurs as to how to ensure accessibility. When we asked a few health administrators doctors associated with AIDS Cell Societies in a few states and discussed the discriminating attitude of doctors, and asked for a possible solution, most of them believed that there is need of increasing the training programmes. When we asked if the fear of punishment could drive doctors to perform their duty ethically and could influence them to treat HIV positive without discrimination[9]? In reply, they mentioned that it is because of fear of infection doctors are not ready to treat HIV positive people. If they would be forced more with fear of punishment then, it may not solve the problem.

Around two-thirds of the total patients who seek treatment for one or other diseases are HIV positive. Therefore, it is difficult for the doctors to avoid such a large number of patients and hence doctors also could be vulnerable (Karmarkar 1999). Thus, sufficient numbers of training programs are required to be arranged for educate the medical community including doctors in matters concerning HIV/AIDS including proper treatment of HIV patients. There is no doubt that many organisations are working in this area of providing and arranging training programs for medical community, but it remains inadequate and also to an extent unsuccessful in covering local doctors. (Karmarkar 1999). Moreover, there is also requirement of awarding the good effort taken by medical community.

For HIV infection, blood contact is one of the means of transmission, keeps medical personnel particularly, doctors, nurses and the medical assistants vulnerable that carries out blood tests. However, use of universal measures during medial practice reduces the chance of the infection to a large extent. But any negligence from the side of the doctors or medical staff also can be fatal. In India, it is a usual practice whereby doctors or medical staffs generally do not use the universal precautionary measures. They are rather habituated to treat a patient even without wearing a glove and other necessary devices. The medical professionals are other wise advised to use the universal precautionary measures to avoid themselves from any type of the infections. But sometimes due to shortage of the necessary items or for less interest, medical staff remains susceptible to some or other infection. Therefore, it is essential from the side of the government to make available all the necessary articles needed for maintaining universal precautionary measures at one hand and on the other hand, it is also necessary on the part of doctors to use such items.

The State government also needs to ensure that all the centres meant for HIV treatment or even the blood banks and other private hospitals provide adequate counselling. In this process, the state may regulate private hospitals. The state also needs to see that while establishing health centres the geographical constraints can be minimised.

Conclusion

The central government as well as state governments have taken many initiatives towards ensuring health rights of people. Several hospitals have been chalked out to provide health care to people. Despite all such initiatives, accessibility of health care has remained a distance dream for many HIV positive people. In Karnataka when the VCTC centres have reached the bloc level, in West Bengal, it is at the district level. Even as far as ART centre is concerned in the state of West Bengal it has created constraints for HIV positive people to access health care. In addition to it, even a few existing health centres in both the state have been denying treatment to HIV positive people. Similarly, many of the health centres provided less emphasis on the counselling that prevented people from accessing information relating their health and gave psychological strength. Case of discrimination has been there within the medical set up. Even cases were found where HIV positive people were discriminated by doctors. Moreover, instances were found where doctors either referred all HIV positive cases to other hospitals or denied treatment.

Such evidences show that the ethical role of the medical profession has been clearly taking a back stage. Several orientation and training courses have been conducted for medical and paramedical staff yet need more such courses. Reward to doctors who treat HIV positive people with great care and punishment to doctors who deny treatment may be tried out simultaneously. The state needs to retrospect its own action and eradicate mistakes and shortcomings relating to its own action. It has to provide required accessories for maintaining universal precautionary measure. In the process the state also may regulate the third party (private health care centres) as it affects the right to accessibility of HIV positive people. It has to ensure that patients in general and HIV positive people in particular are not devoid of health rights. As it is the obligation of state to ensure health rights of people.

REFERENCES

Cheria Anita, Sriprapha Petcharamesree and Edwin. 2004. *A human rights approach to development:* Resource Book, Bangalore: Book for Change.

Karmarkar Santosh. 1999. HIV/AIDS in India: the Last Straw?, *Indian Journal of Medical Ethics,* Apr-Jun 1999-7, (2). (http://www.ijme.in/072ed037.html)

Marks Stephen P. 2004. *The Right to Development: A Primer, Centre for Development and Human Rights,* New Delhi: Sage Publications.

The Times of India. 2007. WHO prescribes HIV testing for All. 02 Jun 2007.

Indiastat. 2009. www.indiastat.com

NOTES

1. As a part of the obligation to respect the State's need to adopt legislation or to take other measures to ensure equal access to health care and services provided by the third parties. The state has to ensure that privatisation of health sector should not be a major thereat to anybody's health rights. Thus, it makes it obligatory for the state to regulate the private health sector.

2. Detected number of AIDS cases or HIV positive cases may not be considered as the exact number. From our observation we came to know that unless people get their tests done they hardly become aware of their health status. For instance, we found men and women both being positive, but their children having not done their HIV tests. For the children the chances of having HIV is more, hence, if we count all such cases and other undetected HV cases then its number will be much more.
3. The universe of HIV/AIDS is either taken as an estimated number or it is often referred as the detected cases. As not all human beings go for HIV test, actual universe of HIV/AIDS remain a mystery to all. Additionally, due to the stigma attached to it, not all HIV patients reveal their status. In such case, either estimation or detected case will not convey the generalisation.
4. The sample size is justified with the help of Central Limit Theorem. It states that 'when the size of the sample increases and becomes sufficiently large the distribution of the sample means tends to Normal Distribution. Here we must take one thing in our notice that the theorem is equally valid for both normal and strongly non-normal. Even if the population distribution is strongly non-normal, its sampling distribution of means tends to normal distribution for "large sample size". A "large sample size" means n > 30 i.e. over 30 (http://www.pinkmonkey.com)
5. In Kolkata, a hospital refused to touch the body of a young AIDS patient who died later. In Indore, a pregnant woman died outside a government hospital without treatment. In Lucknow, a renal failure patient (HIV positive) had to wait for 16 hours before activists could get him a hospital bed (*The Times of India*, 2007).
6. Sulatana got the disease from her husband
7. Universal Precautionary measures help a doctor from the transmission of initial infection. In case of HIV the measures cannot 100 per cent guarantee to check the infection but it reduces the chances of infection. It includes long globes, goggles, different kind of syringe, etc.
8. A group discussion held between ten HIV positive women (who are members of HIV positive network in both the states) made us understand about these problems. We also verified these facts with the respondents during the interview.
9. The idea of punishment to doctors basically who deny treatment came from a few respondents as well as a few other HIV positive people.

Civil Society Approach to Public Health
A Critical Examination

— Kavesher Krishnan

Introduction

The experiences and contributions of Civil Societies particularly those engaged with development activities in the modern era can be traced since 1960's when several development organizations working in the field of education, health care and environment began to posit an alternative development discourse and agenda through their practices.

The current paradigm emphasizing Civil Societies believes on the premise that people can develop themselves, their own involvement, knowledge and contribution is the essential foundation of development. This contrast from the mainstream development discourse, that focuses on growth in GNP and macro-economic development. Thus it is an alternative to the practice of the state.

Theoretical Premise

The term 'Civil Society', so much in vogue today, is an old term, originating as it did with 17th century political philosophers such as Thomas Hobbes and John Locke. The concept assumed sharper focus in Hegel's writings and subsequently in Marx's critique of them, but was thereafter relegated to the background till Gramsci took up this subject in his prison writings.

Hobbes without using the term directly defined Civil Society as a 'liberty of the subject in regulating their actions'. In Locke's conception Civil society has two dimensions. One that it provides redress and security against anarchy and arbitrariness of the 'state of nature' and on the other, through the devolution of legislative powers providing the population security against the arbitrariness of the government.

Hegel's concept of Civil Society which embraces the realm of economic interests, labour, private property and class distinction. He essentially refers to the totality of the material conditions of life while conceding the duality of political society (the state) and civil society (material conditions of life). Hegel lays down that concrete freedom consists in their identity.

Marx and Engels, on the other hand, give an independent identity to Civil Society, that is, they refuse to concede the fundamental identity of the State and Civil Soceity. Marx demands the abolition of the anti-thesis between political society (State) and civil society through the abolition of both. This is to be achieved by the introduction of unrestricted voting as a means to the fullest extension of democracy, which he broadly equates with the transition to socialism.

As mentioned earlier, it is Antonio Gramsci whose writings have created the new interest in civil society and its role and potentialities in contemporary socio-political life. Gramsci's contribution to this concept has two distinct aspects, not explicit in either Hegel or Marx. These are (1) interpenetration of political society and economic society or the state and civil society and (2) a recognizable autonomy of civil society which gives it a distinct space for operation and development. According to him, there are 'two major super structural levels': the one that is called civil society, that is the ensemble of organisms commonly, called 'private' and that of 'political society' or 'the State'.

Most of these theoretical expositions on the origin and development of the concept, civil society traces to challenges the socio-political order of the time. However, of late in practice on all continents, civil societies have made that, civil and political responses to secure rights are inseparable from the economic, social and cultural rights.

In current context, the trends in globalization have affected Civil Societies to diverse countries and situations. Many different analyses have been presented but three common implications seem to engage around the world. First, domestic civil societies have gained greater recognition and visibility as a rightful player in addressing various problems, second, it has emerged as a separate sector and third, in respect of their relations with the state and the market.

As a consequence of an increasing interaction with market institutions, accessing public services for the people and promoting human rights of all without discrimination through consumer movement is the clearest manifestation around the world. Second, greater expectation on Civil Society in aspect of delivery of public services when welfare state restructures itself is observed in basic education, health care, water, sanitation etc. One obvious arena is in the field of SHGs and Micro finance. But the nature of relationship becomes one of the contractor and subcontractor, where voluntary organizations receive payments for fulfilling prescribed targets by the state with the developmental framework.

Third, there has emerged greater demand for and requirements of engaging with global institutions and issues as they impact the lives of their own people. Civil Society organizations are visibly engaging in numerous international conferences of the UN system.

Different Versions

There have been diverse versions and practices of civil societies across globe. Following is the one version, which is something that does not take into account in such perceptions that people are not homogeneous and with diverse interests, ideologies with conflicts of class and caste intricacies.

Civil Society is the manifestation of individual and collective initiatives for common public good. It expresses the interest and aspirations of the people. Civil Society engages with local and national governments (state) to influence policies and access resources. This allows us to look at Civil Society in three different ways. First, Civil society is a space that is free, open and accessible. Therefore it is a space for ideas, for action, for discussion and debate, and for contestation. In this view, civil society is the base arena where values, perspectives and norms are developed, debated, accepted and contested. These can also initiate movements. Civil Society also represents the space where subaltern, hitherto inaudible and unarticulated views can be expressed.

Second, Civil Society can also be seen as a movement for advancing various causes like women rights, health rights, tribal rights, human rights, peace and environment, have all been advanced through a variety of social movements. There are also movements for protest-protest against the policies and actions of powerful national and international institutions that go against dams, displacement and price hikes.

Third, Civil Society can be represented by also a set of organizations. These are primarily self-help, mutual help and support groups. Through them, the families and citizens get together to advance their common public good. Neighborhoods groups, Self help groups, Village councils, Arts and Sports clubs, Water Management Committees and Forest Protection groups are certain examples of such Civil Society organizations. Civil Society also includes strong membership organizations, such as trade unions, cooperatives and social clubs like Rotary club, Red Cross etc. In other words, 'Civil societies are citizens organized, united by common needs, interests, values or traditions and mobilized into many kinds of activity'

UNDP enlists Civil Societies encompassing groups and associations which include, but not limited to, non-governmental organizations, peoples organizations, trade unions, cooperatives, consumer and human right groups, women associations, youth clubs, the media, neighborhood groups, academic and research institutions, grass root movements and organizations of indigenous peoples.

Thus the civil society may be seen as a range of groups and associations (mostly registered) engaged with diverse range of activities to advance their common good. As the paper brings into limelight the civil society engagement on public health, the concerns and limitations depicted are deliberately linked to the development domains without denying of course, that development initiatives are only an arena in the broad range of concerns of Civil Societies.

Civic Society Approach to Public Health

An approach through civil societies to health care offers the opportunity to look at the general crisis of politics in this country too. We cannot achieve a healthier or safer society without widespread civic involvement has been largely neglected by the conventional policy discussions.

The civic nature of public health need has to be understood in a broader framework. First, while acknowledging that the field of biomedicine could not exist without professional practice requiring special training, expertise and committed individual professional practitioners, at the same time nor could it exist without an organized social structure, its citizens support and inter-sectoral collaborations. While looking at the extraordinary technological advances of modern health care, we often tend to forget how 'civic' an achievement this has been. Medical knowledge and practice have taken shape and developed not just by accident, but also because of deliberate public decisions in the form of laws, governmental regulations and public policies.

Civil Society has its own politics. This reminds us of the classical Chadwickian versus Virchow debate. When Virchow emphasized upon poverty reduction to combat the distress and widespread spread of diseases in the filthy industrial towns and cities of Britain as a result of Industrial Revolution, Edward Chadwick move to abolish Elizabethan Poor Law and the Sanitary Reforms took shape in the policy decisions. Also recall that Edward Chadwick is considered the father of Public Health. It depicts the acceptance of dominant group perceptions. Thus civil society groups have their own perceptions but only dominate perceptions (that too not all) takes shape. This reflects in most public health policy decisions.

Secondly, recognizing that health care is intensely private and intimate aspects having potent in seeking care at the moment of ones need of great need, vulnerability and helplessness, it do have ripple effects in the culture and society as a whole when encountered with macro policies. The recent private face of health care bringing systemic issues of efficiency, cost containment and rationing become central to the policy agenda are examples to it. These bring forth challenges of what these changes means to health as a 'public good', which is to be created and sustained through the state and its welfare initiatives.

Seeing health as something that involves us all will be essential for generating widespread consciousness and reworking public views about its concerns affecting populations across.

These domain of significant obstacles to a civic approach, built into the importance of how the health's 'civicness' is conceptualized. However, the paper urges that the policy framers should incorporate the diverse understandings through adequately providing space in the development initiates in the current context.

Engagement with Public Health - Some Concerns

Noting the prominent trends in the current context, that the role of Civil Societies have been widely said to be a complementary partner to state in the development process- this section engages to critically analyze the extent potentials bestowed in civil societies to achieve the development goals in contrast to the state's withdrawal. This feature is overwhelmingly spelt out almost in every policy discourses ranging from national to international documents.

UNDP in its Human Development Report 2001 redefines its responsibilities to build alliances and partnership with civil societies across local and national levels in fulfilling development initiatives. UNDP commits towards making Sustainable Human Development (SHD) and Poverty alleviation possible through civil societies and which it says will complement the role of the state and market. This report has been well received by the civil societies representing the elite and powerful forces in developing and developed countries. UNDP as an institution which seeks a new development paradigm that is an alternative to, or at least distinct from the Structural Adjustment policies of the Bretton-Woods institutions-a new approach that takes account of the role and potential of civil society.

Further the trend reflects National Policy documents too. The National Health Policy 2002 solicits the participation of private and Non-Governmental Organizations (NGOs) as partners in the task of delivery of public health programs. This phenomenon is evident in other documents like the National Water Policy 2002, National Housing Policy etc.

Two apprehensions arise in ones mind when looking at these documents. One is that the role of the welfare state is abdicating from its envisaged development responsibilities and the other that in the name of increased participation of diverse partners in the development programmes, and systemic issues such as efficiency, cost containment and rationing in the form of user charges, private health insurance on social sectors have been made central to the policy agenda. New definitions and principles through management inputs into Public Health on the basis of 'efficiency and effectiveness' arguments been also placed to the center of indicator in public health delivery system.

However, examining the real picture of various forms of civil societies as a complementary partner in fulfilling development tasks provide a dismal picture against the immense trust that they could create before the policy framers.

The inefficiency argument of the state as characterized with inefficient and ill-equipped to handle social sectors including health suggests for an alternative mix of public and private. The primary health care to the government and the lucrative curative care to the private sector is the example to it. And further certain options that fall between completely state oriented services and privatized care. One of the early options is NGOs. As citied by K.R.Nayar, Oliver Razum *et al.,* (2003) that a number of impact studies show that in respect to reaching the poor, coverage and cost-effectiveness, quality of services or policy direction, NGOs do not have any advantage over the state. Without ignoring the organizations inclinations to politics adherence on ideological premise of their operations, it is also observed that as the concentration of funding increases, 'NGOs are susceptible to bureaucratization, self-aggrandization and imposition of standard solutions'.

The limitations of civil societies to influence policies and programmes are due to their lack of 'vision and mission' and unscientific practices. Most organizations fail to substantiate their arguments with adequate data or well-documented reports based on their field experiences. This non-professional ways reflects in their project-oriented approaches and issue based functioning that tends to perceive a narrow outlook rather than a comprehensive framework in these Community Based Organizations (CBOs). In Kerala, the Kerala Shastra

Sahitya Parishad (KSSP) in 1987 succeeded in the collection and analysis of the data on the health habits and health problems of Keralaites in connection with the socio-economic conditions. KSSP, holds the perspective in connection with the holistic development of the society. Thus holding that, 'health is the birth right of the people' this largest Peoples Science Movement (PSM) across the nation since 1962 engaged in struggles that had been against the crisis in modern medicine over its dependency on technology, its urban centered growth, creation of new diseases by medicines, the negation of environmental factors to illness, exploitation by drug companies and its institutionalization and commercialization and furthering encroachment of it on the traditional forms of health systems.

Through its perspectives and activities the KSSP demanded a health policy for Kerala that is based to benefit the majority of the people (KSSP 1992 Dec.d), reconstitution of the medical facilities, decentralization of the administrative and finance pattern, efficient public health services and government hospitals and human resource development in the health sector. But the political inclination of this body could not be ignored mentioning at this context. As KSSP is sidelined today even if they focus on the issues of poor and their conditions because understood to be adhering to Marxism.

Most Civil Societies function on a compact and compartmentalized fashion with distinct identity in furtherance of their own interests at the grass root level. This hurdles in building both horizontal and vertical networking in the broader developmental frame. Furthermore, who will coordinate these organizations for the common issue at a broader platform they hail for?

Even though, the civil societies at the grass root operations perceived to be people-oriented and reflects the wishes and wills, aims and aspirations of the people's felt need-added with their inclination to local politics, its has dangers of 'localism'. By focusing so heavily on the 'the local' the see manifestations tend to underplay both local inequalities and power relations as well as national and transnational economic and political forces. Thus advocating a stronger emphasis on the politics of local, ie, on the political use of 'the local' the hegemonic and counter-hegemonic interests play prominently. This manifestation is observed while looking into the key political arenas like decentralized service delivery participatory development (issues cited elsewhere in this paper), social capital formation and local development and collective actions for 'radical democracy'.

This phenomenon of local elites and dominance is very well reflected in the interplays of Village Council or Gramasabha, Forest Management Committees, Water Management Committees etc. The experience of Democratic decentralization in Kerala provide cases of female headed Panchayath President reflecting the stories of husbands or any other close relatives who anchor the local politics and hurdle genuine decision making process.

Conventionally, Public Health commitment of diverse civil societies confine to the elements of information provider alone. The HIV/AIDS awareness, Environment awareness campaigns, Awareness on the ill-effects of Alcoholism and Drug abuse run across education institutions, community centres, rural libraries supported by national agencies such as Central Social Welfare Board (CSWB), Department of Science and Technology (DST) and the Department of Publicity and Advertisements are regular features of this phenomena. These aspects are picturised as a commitment towards 'social cause' element in the activities of Trade Unions, Residential Associations, Youth and Arts Clubs, Rural libraries etc. The National AIDS Control Organization (NACO) sets a major chunk of its project fund on processing, development and display of Information Education and Communication (IEC) component ignoring the structural issues on the causation of STD/HIV/AIDS on its targeted population.

Moreover, this wholesome commitment could be weighed in terms of the fund (both foreign and domestic) these civil societies could pool out. Rotary Clubs engage in construction of sanitary latrines or the Church based organizations engage in community based rehabilitation initiatives are predominantly determined by their respective funding partner rather than their genuine need generated from the field.

Self-help groups provide psycho-social support and information (prevention and promotion) to patients and limited form of Primary health care, is often determined by a predetermined framework reflecting a project approach in it. The WHO Report on Macroeconomic and Health (2002) identified health as an effective instrument for reducing poverty in low-income countries. With their social and health systems cash-strapped, Self-help is being proposed as an allegedly less costly but effective means of improving population health. Studies provide diverse range of other limitations with SHG approaches too. There is a broad agreement that SHGs cannot replace existing professional health services, but complement them. Another reason is that they are not equally appropriate in all population strata. Largely middle class in distant middle class suburbs runs many groups. Males, minorities, the aged, the aged, the working and lower classes are under-represented. Overall only 6-9% of potential participants actually engage in Self-help activities.

Further, it needs to be noted that mostly SHGs are steered from the outsiders (by politicians or health experts). Chief reason for its failure is the autocratic leadership style of founders and a bureaucratization that prelude in its membership participation. Most often governmental funding accelerates their process-which loses necessary autonomy and self-determination and are appropriated and instrumentalised by state planning. The same happens when professional try to influence them. In the functioning of

SHGs, while mutual respect and cooperation can be productive, competitive for clients status and power may arise.

The value of recognizing and involving the intended beneficiaries of public health programmes throughout all phases of programme planning, implementation and evaluation is called in the recent years. This community-based participatory public health programmes brings on challenges to those civil societies engaged in community-based interventions. The competencies of such participatory approaches should enable them to (1) enhance the capacity of the community members to serve in partnership endeavors (2) Appreciate the role of participation by the under-represented and underserved population and (3) develop skills for mobilizing community resources to address community defined priorities. But most often it is observed that, such participatory processes generates expectations among the people and harms the serving environment of such organizations in the field. And further these participatory techniques are administered keeping in a preoccupied bias of externally motivated fund raising purpose and within the rigid conditionality frame of the funding partners. The issue of 'outsider' and 'insider' debate in seeking participation cannot be ignored in such approaches. The classical instance of Qadeer, Imrana study on CHW (Community Health Workers) on the Shandol District in Maharastra State provide insights on how within the community the CHW experiences outsider across various social groups.

Before conclusion, the much controversial ethical and non-ethical debate within civil societies and across disciplines of biomedicine and social sciences need to be pointed. The ethical phenomenon is a relative concept and the 'ethical' in me may not be so to others. The field of Public Health in the civil society too passes through such dilemma. Due to such reasons the Church based organizations do not engage with issues of HIV/AIDS interventions among targeted populations like sex workers, MSMs etc. The technological face of biomedicine will ignore the interactive quality element of patients. A technology with human face takes long path of agreement upon coming to a common consensus.

Conclusions

The strengths and weakness in entrusting public health tasks to civil societies face multifarious hurdles across the real development arena. The concerns described in the paper provide only a narrow edge of a broad iceberg touching only certain elementary issues one normally encounters in the day-today situations of development.

Meanwhile, recognizing the potential of concerted actions of civil societies from the lessons they draw from popular movements in their long struggles, certain critical qualms need also to be further examined. One is that which are these newly emerged forms of civil societies? Are they genuinely engaged in the empowering relationships to promote so called 'people centered development'? Do they represent the voiceless, unreachable or socially excluded groups in their society? If so, what is the nature of such relationships with these groups- are they representing 'for' or 'of' those groups? Further and foremost, the nature of politics in these civil society functioning- Don't these engage in politics to secure their positions in the development framework?

However, the paper does not ignore the element of politics in public health but cautions to the extend of politicking (manipulation or articulation of dominant views in the name of fair politics).

Therefore from these qualms it is apparent from these examinations that the space for authentic civil societies is missed out along when the state also is abdicating its welfare responsibilities furthering to the vulnerability, marginalisation and bringing minimum options and choices to the voiceless, inaudible and inarticulate groups in the society.

REFERENCES

Craig, G: 1984. Work and the State, *Community Development Journal*. pp. 3-18.

Gramsci, Antonio; 1973. *Selections from Prison*, New Books: Edited and Translated by Q. Hoare and G.N. Smith, International Publishers, New York, p. 12.

Hobbes, Thomas*; Man and the State - The Political Philosophy*. Modern Pocket Library. Kaldor, Mary. *et al.* 2003. Global Civil Society, Oxford

Kannan K.P *et al.* 1991. *Health Studies in Rural Kerala*; KSSP Study.

Katz A.H. 1981. Self Help and Mutual Aid: An emerging social Movement? *Annual Review of Sociology*. No 7; pp. 129-155.

Locke, M. 1986. The fourth estate in Medicine? *British Medical Journal* (Clinical research Ed.); pp.1596-1600.

Marx and Engels. 1964. *The German ideology*. Progressive Publishers, Moscow, p.48.

Marx, Karl. 1967 *Writings of the Young Marx on Philosophy and Society*. 1967. Translated and Edited by D. Easton and Kurt.H, Anchor Books, New York, p. 116.

Mohan, Giles and Kristian Stoke. 2000. Participatory Development and Empowerment: the dangers of Localism, *Third World Quarterly*, Vol. 21. No. 2; pp. 247-268.

Nancy Kari et.al. 1994. Health as a Civic Question, prepared for *American Civic Forum*, Internet.

Nayar K.R, Oliver Razum et.al. 2004. Int. Journal of Equity in Health; Self help: *What future role in health Care for Low and Middle income Countries?*

Parker, Edith *et al.,* 2003. Assessing the capacity of Health Departments engage in Community based Participatory Public health; *American Journal of Public Health*; Vol. 93; No. 3.

Roy, Ajith. 1995. Civil Society and Nation State - In Contrast of Globalization. *EPW*. No.1. Aug 2008.

Salamon, *et al.* 2003. *Global Civil Society: An Overview*, The John Hopkins University, USA. Internet

Tandon, Rajesh and Mohanty, Ranjita, 2003: *Does Civil Society Matters*? Governance in Contemporary, India. Sage Publication, India

Tandon, Rajesh, 2002. *Voluntary Action, Civil Society and the State.* Mosaic Books, India.

Tandon, Rajesh. 1994. Globalising Civil Society; Continuity and Change; Keynote Address delivered at JANPORA, Japan on Mar 2004; as quoted from CIVICUS: World Alliance for Citizen Participation, Citizens: Strengthening Global Civil Society.

The Report on an Inquiry into the Sanitary Conditions of Labouring Populations of Great Britain; 1842. Edwin Chadwick.

UNDP Human Development Report, 2001.

UNDP, Human Development Report 2001; Civil Society, NGDOs and Sustainable Development, Occasional Paper 1.

Varughese, Shiju Sam. 2002. Ideological Premise of KSSP as a Peoples Science Movement; M.Phil Dissertation to CSP (SSS), JNU.

Wolfe. M. 1994. Some Integration: Institutions and Actors. Occasional Paper No. 4. World Summit for Social Development.

World Bank; Human Development Report; Investing in Health, Washington; 1993.

CHAPTER

Study of Spatial Disparity in Maternal and Child Health Care Services among the States of Indian Union

— Dr. Aditya Kumar Patra and Arbinda Acharya

ABSTRACT

Safe motherhood practice and child survival programmes are critically important in a country like India experiencing high infant mortality and maternal mortality. Attempt has been made in this write-up to examine the spatial disparities in maternal and child health facilities across 14 major states of India over time and in turn analyses its impact on maternal and child mortality rate. This research article proposes simple multivariate method to compute composite indices of maternal health care and child health care. Empirical evidence suggests that there is wide spread inter-state variation of these index values. On the one end southern states in general, Kerela and Tamil Nadu in particular are well improved states, on the other end BIMARU (Bihar, Madhya Pradesh, Rajasthan and Uttar Pradesh) states depict a dismal picture.

Preface

Maternal and Child Health Services are one of the basic health services to be provided by any government health system as pregnant women and child are one of the most vulnerable victims of dysfunctional health system. India, in spite of rapid economic progress is still far away from the goal of lowering maternal mortality to less than 100 per

100,000 live births and infant mortality rate below 30 per 1000 live birth. The maternal mortality ratio (MMR) and infant mortality rate (IMR) in India varies across the states. Geographical vastness and socio-cultural diversity make implementation of health sector reforms a difficult task. This write up analyses the trends in maternal mortality ratio and infant mortality rate across the states along with various maternal and child health programs implemented over the years.

Introduction

Health and socio-economic developments of any country are interdependent. Yet the economic development in India has gained momentum over the last decade, but the public health system is lagging behind. India has high maternal mortality ratio at 301 and infant mortality rate of 58. Most of the developed countries have low maternal and child mortality rates compared to developing nations. Certain developing nations placed in almost similar situation such as Indonesia, Sri Lanka and China have performed much better than India (Table 9.1).

Table 9.1 : Health Indicators among Selected Countries

Country	IMR (per 1000 live births)	MMR (per 100000 live births)
India	58	301
China	32	56
Japan	3	10
Republic of Korea	3	20
Indonesia	36	230
Malaysia	9	41
Vietnam	27	130
Bangladesh	52	380
Nepal	58	740
Pakistan	73	500
Sri Lanka	15	92

Source: Eleventh Plan, Volume 2, pp.58, PC, GoI

In India the MMR during 2001-03 has been 301 per 100000 live births. Levels of maternal mortality vary across the states (Table 9.2). The rural maternal mortality ratio is considerably higher than the urban area. This difference of maternal mortality ratio is basically due to difference in access to emergency obstetric care (EmOC), prenatal care, anemia among women, education level of women, etc. As per SRS data about 38 per cent of women are estimated to die from hemorrhage, mostly post partum hemorrhage. Within "other conditions", anemia is found to be the main medical condition leading to maternal death. Anemia is common in reproductive age due to various socioeconomic and demographic reasons such as low status of women, lack of access to good nutrition, high fertility and short gap between births (Figure 9.1).

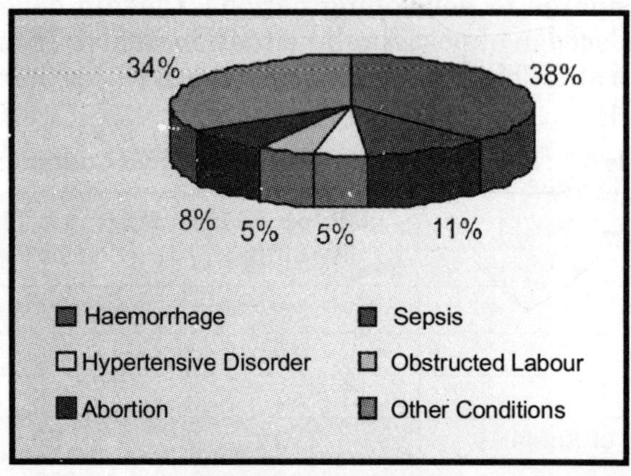

Fig. 9.1 : Inter-State Variation of Maternal Health Care Services over Time

Data show that infant mortality rate in India is 58 per 1000 live birth. It is higher in rural areas of the country and varies across states (Table 9.2). IMR depends on vaccination coverage and pre- post-natal maternal health services. Over the decades there has been a declining trend in infant mortality rate. Various causes of infant mortality are diarrhea, acute respiratory infection (ARI), sepsis, asphyxia, premature birth, etc. (Figure 9.2).

Table 9.2 : Inter-State Variation of MMR & IMR

	Infant Mortality Rate			Maternal Mortality Ratio			
	NFHS 1	NFHS 2	NFHS 3	SRS 2007	SRS 1998	SRS 2001	SRS 2003
Andhra Pradesh	70.4	65.8	53.5	54	151	176	148
Bihar	89.2	72.9	61.7	58	651	549	486
Gujarat	68.7	62.6	49.7	52	52	199	166
Haryana	73.3	56.8	41.7	55	161	190	169
Karnataka	65.4	51.5	43.2	47	225	229	189
Kerela	23.8	16.3	15.3	13	92	93	66
Madhya Pradesh	85.2	86.1	69.5	72	554	534	474
Maharashtra	50.5	43.7	37.5	34	172	138	117
Odisha	112.1	81.0	64.7	71	297	367	295
Punjab	53.7	57.1	41.7	43	244	144	138
Rajasthan	72.6	80.4	65.3	65	647	655	561
Tamil Nadu	67.7	48.2	30.4	35	89	115	88
Uttar Pradesh	99.9	86.7	72.7	69	867	772	700
West Bengal	75.3	48.7	48	37	251	175	148

Source: NFHS I, 2 & 3, IIPS, Mumbai; SRS Bulletin 1998, 2001, 2003 & 2007.

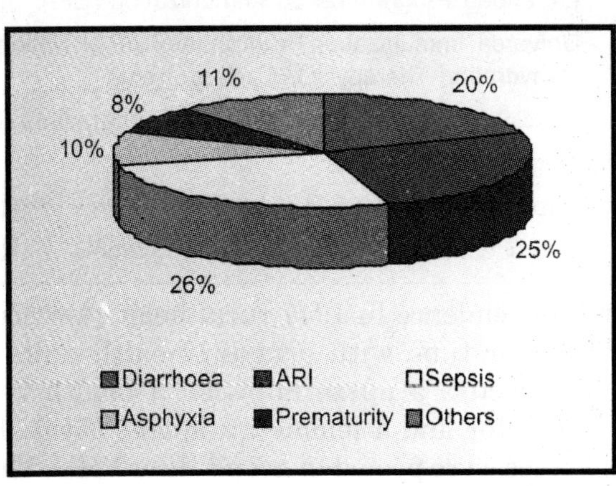

Fig. 9.2 : Causes of Infant Mortality in India

Two of the goals set by the Eleventh Five-year Plan for the year 2012 are to reduce the infant mortality rate (IMR) at 28 per 1000 live births and maternal mortality ratio (MMR) to one maternal death per 1000 live birth. Hence, concerted effort is essential to reduce both the MMR and IMR to the targeted level.

Evolution of MCH Programmes in India

At the time of India's independence, health care services in India were scant, predominantly urban, hospital based, & curative. The National Family Planning Program was launched in 1952 with emphasis on population control. The maternal and child health (MCH) programme has evolved over a period of time (Box 1).

Box 1: Evolution of Maternal and Child health programmes in India

1952:	Family Planning Programme adopted by Govt. of India (GOI)
1961:	Dept. of Family Planning created in Ministry of Health
1971:	Medical Termination of Pregnancy Act (MTP Act) 1971
1977:	Renaming of Family Planning to Family Welfare
1978:	Expanded Programme on Immunization (EPI)
1985:	Universal Immunization Programme (UIP) + National Oral Rehydration Therapy (ORT) Programme
1992:	Child Survival and Safe Motherhood Programme (CSSM)
1996:	Target -free approach
1997:	Reproductive and Child Health Programme -1 (RCH-1)
2005:	Reproductive and Child Health Programme -2 (RCH-2)

After Independence in 1947 rural health services were established over time with primary health units (PHU) staffed by a doctor, a nurse midwife, a health visitor, a sanitary inspector and a female attendant (Aya). Trained nurse midwives were posted in hospitals or PHU. Their role in PHUs was to conduct deliveries and visit a population of

10,000. Sub-centers were established below PHUs to provide basic medical care and delivery care at the field level. To place trained personnel in this newly instituted health centers, temporary workers with preliminary education were trained for shorter time and recruit at sub centres. These workers were called "Auxiliary Nurse Midwife" (ANMs) Auxiliary workers are technical workers in a particular field with less than full qualifications (WHO 1961). Shetty committee suggested training auxiliary nurses and midwives for short time to work under supervision for specific duties. Twelve training centres were established by 1954 to fulfill the requirements. Later on committees such as Bhore and Mudaliar suggested continuation of auxiliary cadre to provide basic health care at field level. Hence, ANMs gradually became permanent staff in public health system.

National programmes have shifted the focus from comprehensive reproductive health services to preventive services. In the mid 60s family planning was integrated with MCH activities and projected as a program deserving the highest priority (GOI, Planning Commission 1968). A separate department and structures of family planning were created at the central, state and district levels with the sole function of promoting family planning through the PHC staff. This created an impression that the staffs funded by family planning (FP) program was to restrict themselves to only FP activities whereas in theory all the Sub centres and PHC doctors had similar job descriptions which included MCH too. The new ANMs employed under the FP program did not feel the need to stay at sub centre (SC) Village since their work did not relate to any emergencies such as childbirth.

During mid 80s the immunization program called the Expanded Program for Immunization (EPI) for children below five years started to receive priority. The implementation of the program at field level was assigned to the ANM. EPI was followed by Universal Immunization Programme (UIP), again supported by UNICEF. The National Child

Survival and Safe Motherhood Programme (CSSM) developed by Government of India and supported by World Bank and UNICEF was to provide child survival and safe motherhood services through the PHC system in India. It started in 1992 as follow up to the Universal Immunization Program. There were eight goals of the programme out of which one was for maternal health viz., reduction of maternal mortality from 4 to 2 per 1000 births. Although the package specified care at birth as a service, the work plan of the ANM at the sub centre level did not specify conducting deliveries in the list of critical activities. Similarly this was missing from the module for planning MCH services at the PHC and SC level and the sample work plan of the ANM given in the workers' manual. Unknowingly the program created a conceptual conflict through its fixed day schedule by giving more priority to routine preventive services compared to emergency services.

Following the International Conference on Population and Development, 1994, the government started the process of reorienting the family planning and maternal child health programmes into a new program called the Reproductive Child Health I (RCH I). The World Bank's sector review and project appraisal document show that a lot of background work and thinking had gone into the development of the program. To provide skilled care at birth, the RCH programme incorporated additional nursing staff for primary health centres for round the clock maternal health services and incentives for institutional deliveries. Both these programs had too many components on maternal and child health for which the government health system was not equipped.

In 2005, with World Bank and other donors assistance RCH-2 was started. RCH 2 (2005-2012) again has many components and it revives unsuccessful strategies such as village level volunteers (Accredited Social Health Activist -

ASHA). The 7-year phase of RCH II has launched with a vision to bring about outcomes as envisioned in the Millennium Development Goals, the National Population Policy 2000 (NPP 2000), the Tenth Plan (2007-2010), the National Health Policy 2002 and Vision 2020 India, minimizing the regional variations in the areas of RCH and population stabilization through an integrated, focused, participatory programme meeting the unmet demands of the target population, and provision of assured, equitable, responsive quality services. RCH-2 has also given more flexibility to states to develop strategies appropriate for them. RCH-2 is implemented under National Rural Health Mission (NRHM) which has led to decentralization and increased powers to field level workers. NRHM is an initiative to bring all health programs under one umbrella to improve implementation and monitoring. NRHM provides a thrust for reduction of child and maternal mortality and reduction of fertility rates. Efforts are being made to provide quality Reproductive Health services (including delivery, safe abortions, treatment of reproductive tract infections and family planning services to meet unmet needs, while ensuring full reproductive choices to women).

The main strategy for maternal mortality reduction of the government focuses on safe/institutional deliveries in the governmental and non-governmental sectors under NRHM. Efforts to develop competencies needed for Skilled Birth Attendants (SBAs) in the entire cadre of staff nurses and ANMs will be undertaken. Regular training of select medical officers to administer anesthesia has been taken up. Also multi skill training of medical officers, ANMs and para-medical staffs is to be initiated to close specialist skill gaps. Intensified IEC is to be pursued to ensure behavioural changes that relate to better maternal survival and women's health i.e. spacing, age at marriage, education of the girl child. Community Health Centres (CHCs) are being upgraded to First Referral Units (FRUs) for providing referral services to the mother and child and taking care of obstetric emergencies and complications for provision of safe abortion services and for prevention, testing / counselling in respect of HIV AIDS. Reduction in MMR / IMR will also be closely monitored through social audit, which is being introduced at the village level.

The philosophy behind the strategies to reduce maternal and child mortality under the RCH-II programme is to introduce those interventions that have been proven to be effective in field conditions. Focus is on increasing the deliveries attended by skilled birth attendants in community and more specifically at institutional levels by training the MOs, ANMs/LHVs, improving access to emergency obstetric care by operationalizing of FRUs, training and empowerment of health personnel and the development of sound referral linkages.

Inter-State Variation of Maternal and Child Health Care

In this section we shall examine the variation of maternal and child health care facilities across states over time. The entire period of analysis is divided into three phases, coterminous with NFHS 1 (1992-93), NFHS 2 (1998-99) and NFHS 3 (2005-06). In the present write-up an attempt has been made to construct two Composite Indices: Index of Maternal Health Care (IMHC) and Index of Child Health Care (ICHC) pertaining to different states. We have selected eight indicators pertaining to preventive, promotive and curative health services related to maternity and child health care. The detail list of the parameters is as follows:

Maternal Health Care Indicators

1. Percentage of women who had at least one Anti Natal Care (ANC) visits.
2. Percentage of women who had received 2 or more TT Injection during pregnancy.

3. Percentage of women who took IFA for at least 90 days.
4. Percentage of births delivered in a health facility.
5. Percentage of deliveries assisted by health personnel.

Child Health Care Indicators

6. Percentage of child that received all the recommended doses of vaccinations.
7. Percentage of children with diarrhoea taken to a health provider.
8. Percentage of Children with acute respiratory infection (ARI) taken to a health provider.

Data

For assessing disparities among states with regard to maternal and child health care services in India we have collected information from various rounds of National Family Health Survey (NFHS). Till date National Family Health Survey was conducted thrice in India. The first survey refers to the year 1992-93 followed by a second in 1998-99 and the latest one is the NFHS-3, 2005-06. This survey is a store house of data for a number of health indicators on national and states level separately. The survey is modeled after the 'Demographic and Health Survey' conducted in many countries in world. The survey used pre-tested scientific sampling designs. Hence, the quality of data obtained from the survey is beyond doubt.

Methodology

The methodology adopted for the construction of Composite Indices of maternal and child health care is quite analogous with the Human Development Index of UNDP. The detail methodology runs as follow:

Let X_{ij} represent the value of the ith health parameter in jth state, (i = 1, 2, 3, . . ., 10; j = 1, 2, . . ., 5). Let us write

$$Y_{ij} = \frac{X_{ij} - Min_j X_{ij}}{Max_j X_{ij} - Min_j X_{ij}} \qquad (9.1)$$

Where, $Min_j X_{ij}$ and $Max_j X_{ij}$ are the minimum and maximum of X_{ij} respectively. However, if X_{ij} is negatively associated with the status of health care services, equation (9.1) can be written as:

$$Y_{ij} = \frac{Max_j X_{ij} - X_{ij}}{Max_j X_{ij} - Min_j X_{ij}} \qquad (9.2)$$

Obviously, the scaled dimension index values, Y_{ij}, vary from zero to one.

In all parameters no normal or goal post value has been defined. The observed maximum value of parameters has been taken as the goal post value and observed minimum value is taken as the minimum.

From the matrix of scaled dimension values, Y = {(Y ij)}, we may construct the Composite Indices of different states as:

$$Y_j = \sum_{i=1}^{n} W_i Y_{ij} \qquad (9.3)$$

Where, W is are weights. Here we assign equal weight to all the parameters.

To examine the variation over time indices have been calculated for 1998-99 and 2005-06 by taking 1992-93 as the base value. The indices have been moderated to ignore any negative values and a value greater than one. Zero and one have been substituted for theses respectively (the index value could be negative if the parameter value is less than the minimum of the base year values. Similarly, index value could be greater than one if the parameter value is more than the maximum of the base year value).

The calculated Composite Indices of Maternal and Child Health Care for different states in various points of time are summarized in Table 9.3. From this table it is clear that the index of maternal health care of different states have been improved over time. However, there is a lot of variation of index across the States. On the one end the index value is very low for the state Bihar i.e., 0.032 in initial phase to 0.234 in the 3rd phase and on the other extreme Kerala exhibits a value close to 1 even in the initial phase. Kerela is followed by Tamil Nadu, Andhra Pradesh and Maharastra in the field of maternal health care services. BIMARU states on the other hand depicts dismal picture (Figure 9.3).

Table 9.3 : Composite Index of Maternal Health Care

State	Index Value			Rank		
	NFHS1	NFHS2	NFHS3	NFHS1	NFHS2	NFHS3
Andhra Pradesh	0.620	0.763	0.817	3	3	3
Bihar	0.032	0.145	0.234	14	13	14
Gujarat	0.517	0.665	0.746	7	7	6
Haryana	0.385	0.476	0.617	9	10	10
Karnataka	0.607	0.699	0.775	6	5	5
Kerela	0.999	0.988	1.058	1	1	1
Madhya Pradesh	0.223	0.313	0.484	11	11	11
Maharashtra	0.620	0.736	0.816	4	4	4
Odisha	0.273	0.502	0.661	10	9	9
Punjab	0.618	0.690	0.726	5	6	7
Rajasthan	0.036	0.256	0.469	13	12	12
Tamil Nadu	0.856	0.962	1.027	2	2	2
Uttar Pradesh	0.094	0.142	0.366	12	14	13
West Bengal	0.466	0.647	0.724	8	8	8

Source: Calculated by the Author.

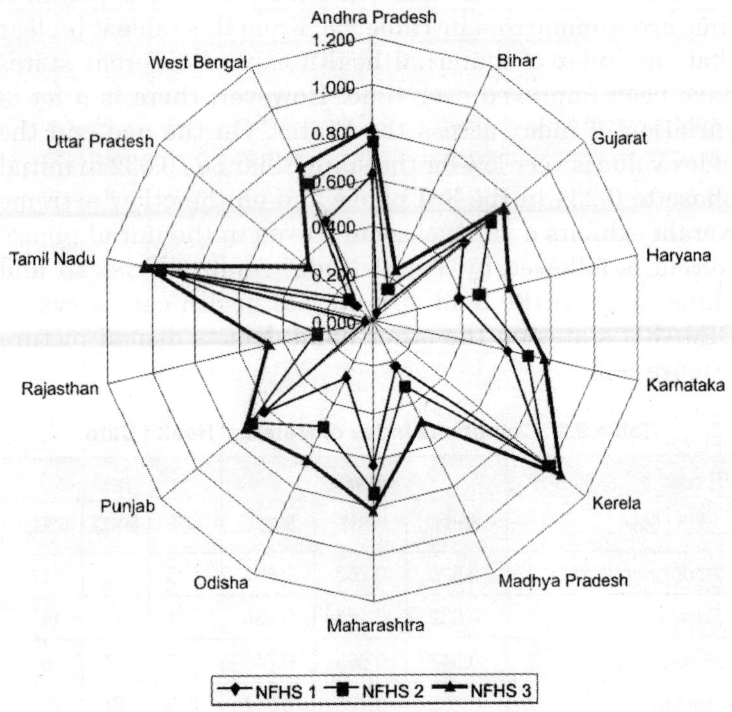

Fig. 9.3 : Inter-State Variation of Maternal Health Care Services over Time

Table 9.4 represents the Composite Index of Child Health Care Services across the states over time. This table depicts the trend and variation of index values among States. In Haryana the position of Child Health Care Service is constantly improve its position over time. The state of Haryana is followed by Kerela, Punjab and Tamil Nadu. However, the position of Madhya Pradesh, Rajasthan, Bihar and Uttar Pradesh with respect to Child Health Care Service the situation is very precarious for entire period of analysis. The position of Odisha improves considerably from a low of 0.177 to 0.573. It has improved its rank from 13 to 8 among 14 states under consideration (Figure 9.4).

Table 9.4 : Composite Index of Child Health Care

State	Index Value			Rank		
	NFHS 1	NFHS 2	NFHS 3	NFHS 1	NFHS 2	NFHS 3
Andhra Pradesh	0.485	0.632	0.415	9	7	9
Bihar	0.282	0.069	0.352	12	14	12
Gujarat	0.561	0.564	0.382	6	8	10
Haryana	0.706	0.984	0.965	3	2	1
Karnataka	0.600	0.710	0.575	5	6	7
Kerela	0.737	0.969	0.877	2	4	2
Madhya Pradesh	0.336	0.213	0.249	11	12	14
Maharashtra	0.628	0.973	0.727	4	3	5
Odisha	0.177	0.230	0.573	13	11	8
Punjab	0.982	1.000	0.868	1	1	3
Rajasthan	0.101	0.198	0.283	14	13	13
Tamil Nadu	0.529	0.936	0.778	7	5	4
Uttar Pradesh	0.354	0.263	0.361	10	9	11
West Bengal	0.518	0.246	0.650	8	10	6

Source: Calculated by the Author.

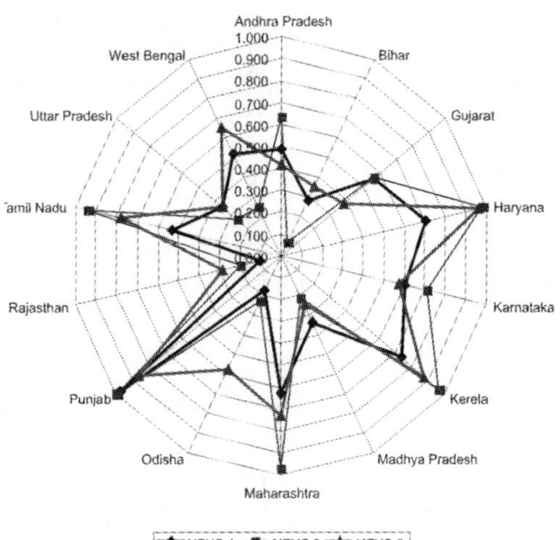

Fig. 9.4 : Inter-State Variation of Child Health Care Services over Time

Socio-cultural Determinants of MCH

The socio-cultural determinants of maternity and child health care have a cumulative effect on maternal mortality rate and infant mortality ratio. Poverty and illiteracy have a negative bearing on the maternal and child health. The female literacy rate in India is 54.3 per cent and 26.1 per cent of the total population in India are below the poverty line. Lack of education particularly female education has an important bearing on age of marriage, knowledge about family planning, availing the benefit of maternal health facilities and protects children from health hazards. Table 5 Explains how low level of education and incidence of poverty

Table 5: Teenage Pregnancy and Infant Mortality Rate

Background Characteristics	Percentage who are pregnant with 1st child	Percentage who have child bearing	Infant Mortality rate
Education (Mother's)			
No Education	6.6	32.6	69.7
< 5 years completed	5.1	21.2	66.0
5-7 years completed	4.7	19.6	49.5
8-9 years completed	2.4	8.5	41.5
10-11 years completed	2.4	6.1	36.5
12 or more years completed	1.6	3.6	25.9
Wealth Index			
Lowest	6.0	25.3	70.4
Second	4.5	21.9	68.5
Middle	3.7	16.3	58.3
Fourth	13.5	11.7	44.0
Highest	1.8	5.1	29.2

Source: NFHS 3, India Report, Volume 1, IIPS, Mumbai

leads to teen age motherhood and high infant mortality rate. Teen age mother hood and early child bearing has no doubt resulted in adverse health consequences, including damage to the reproductive tract, maternal mortality, pregnancy complications, perinatal and neonatal mortality and low birth weight (Kulkarni, 2003). The level of teenage pregnancy and motherhood is 9 times higher among women with no education than among women with 12 or more years of education. Likewise the level of teenage pregnancy and motherhood is 5 times as high for women in households with the lowest wealth index than for women in households with the highest wealth index. It is seen that infant mortality rate decreases steadily with an increase in mother's schooling. The IMR is 70 for children whose mothers having no schooling compared with 26 for children whose mothers have 12 or more years of schooling. Analogously, the infant mortality rate is 70 among children in households in the lowest wealth quintile, 58 in middle wealth quintile households and only 29 in the highest wealth quintile households.

Maternal education and economic status also impacts access to maternal health care. As seen in Table 9.6 mothers and women from lowest wealth quintile have reduced access to basic maternal health care. Only 18 per cent of illiterate mothers had institutional delivery as compared to 86 per cent in mothers with 12 or more years of education. Same difference is seen for post natal care. Women from low economic status have 13 per cent institutional delivery compared to 84 per cent for highest wealth quintile. Same situation is prevalent for post natal care where only 19 per cent of mothers of lowest wealth quintile avail post natal care compared to 79 per cent for highest wealth quintile.

Hence, it is seen from preceding analysis that maternal mortality rate and infant mortality ratio are more affected by socio-economic-cultural factors than the medical / health factors. Therefore efforts should be directed towards improvement of female education and economic empowerment of women to have a dent over MMR & IMR.

Table 5: Teenage Pregnancy and Infant Mortality Rate

Background Characteristics	Antenatal care	Institutional delivery	Deliveries conducted by skilled persons	Postnatal check-up
Education (Mother's)				
No Education	62.0	18.4	26.1	23.6
< 5 years completed	82.4	36.3	45.0	39.8
5-7 years completed	87.0	47.9	56.9	49.7
8-9 years completed	91.4	57.7	67.1	56.0
10-11 years completed	95.0	72.2	80.3	70.3
12 or more years completed	98.3	86.4	91.0	82.8
Wealth Index				
Lowest	58.7	12.7	19.4	19.3
Second	69.2	23.5	31.8	27.7
Middle	80.1	39.2	49.0	42.9
Fourth	90.0	57.9	67.2	56.8
Highest	97.3	83.7	88.8	79.3

Source: NFHS 3, India Report, Volume 1, IIPS, Mumbai

Conclusion

This write-up proposes a simple multivariate method to compute composite indices of maternal health care services and child health care services by combining various maternal and child health service indicators across the states over time. Empirical evidence shows that southern states Andhra Pradesh, Kerela and Tamil Nadu are well ahead of Bihar, Madhya Pradesh, Rajasthan and Uttar Pradesh in the field of Maternal Health Care Services. However, in the area of Child Health Care Services Haryana tops the list followed by Kerela, Punjab and Tamil Nadu. BIMARU states repeat the story as in the former case. Moreover, there exists wide scale inter-state variation of maternal / child health care services. Hence, effort should be directed to provide adequate maternal and child health services along with socio-economic measures to reduce maternal mortality rate and infant mortality ratio.

REFERENCES

Government of India, Planning Commission. *Eleventh Five Year Plan (2007-2012)* Volume II Chapter 4

Government of India, Planning Commission. *Tenth Five Year Plan (2002-2007)* Volume II Chapter 2

Government of India, *Lessons from RCH Phase I, RCH Phase II National Program Implementation Plan*, Ministry of Health & Family Welfare, New Delhi

Government of India. *Maternal mortality in India: 1997-2003 Trends, Causes and Risk Factors*. Registrar General, New Delhi, India

Iyer A., Jesai A. et al, 1995, Women in Health Care: Auxiliary Nurse Midwives. The Foundation for Research in Community Health

Kulkarni S, 2003. The reproductive health status of married adolescents as assessed by IIPS, ORC MACRO, India. In S.Bott et al., eds., *Towards Adulthood: Exlporing the Sexual and Reproductive Health of Adolescents of South Asia:* 55-58. Geneva: WHO

National Family Health Survey-1 (1992-93), India Report, International Institute for Population Sciences, Mumbai, 1995

National Family Health Survey-2 (1998-99), *India Report*, International Institute for Population Sciences, Mumbai, 2000

National Family Health Survey-3(2005-06), *India Report*, Volume I, International Institute for Population Sciences, Mumbai, 2007

National Rural Health Mission Framework for Implementation 2005-2012. Ministry of Health & Family Welfare. New Delhi

The World Bank, 1997, Implementation Completion Report, India. Child Survival and Safe Motherhood Project. The World Bank, Washington D.C. USA.

CHAPTER

Problems of Mental Health

Alarming to the Civil Society

— **Rajib Lochan Panigrahy**

ABSTRACT

Generally problems of health indicated the problems of physical health, i.e. inner and outer parts of the body which is called as disease. But, there is another health which is mental health. The person is under the control of mental health. If mental health is sound, the person is sound in physical health and accordingly his works and duties. If mental health is in disorder, vulnerable, disturbed the capabilities, capacities, work and duties will be disturbed or in trouble or cannot be possible. Now-a-days, the environmental, social, economic, political factors are mostly affecting the mental health of the people which became alarming. From a survey it is find that by 2020, if the present of mental disorder will continue, there will be 40% of the world population affected. It will be a disaster to the civil society. Presently it is seen that the social disturbances, suicidal deaths, madness, depressions, etc. are increasing day by day which increases social and family disturbances. I need the reforms like self-control, yoga, spiritual and healthy environment, nutritious food with natural manure and without pesticides and fertilisers, less use of chemicals and medicines, socialistic pattern of society than the capitalistic form of government, low range of gap in economic standards of the people in the society where s/he is living or organization where s/he is working, etc. Alcoholism, sexual disturbances, gender bios, work culture, cooperation or help at emergencies, mental disorder of different age group, un/dis-employment, lack of social support, behavioural problem, etc. are the man made factors of mental health problems.

Introduction

Mental health refers to our cognitive, and/or emotional well-being - it is all about how we think, feel and behave. Mental health, if somebody has it, can also mean an absence of a mental disorder. Approximately 25% of people in the UK have a mental health problem during their lives. The USA is said to have the highest incidence of people diagnosed with mental health problems in the developed world. Your mental health can affect your daily life, relationships and even your physical health. Mental health also includes a person's ability to enjoy life - to attain a balance between life activities and efforts to achieve psychological resilience.

According to Medilexicon's medical dictionary, mental health is:

> "emotional, behavioral, and social maturity or normality; the absence of a mental or behavioral disorder; a state of psychological well-being in which one has achieved a satisfactory integration of one's instinctual drives acceptable to both oneself and one's social milieu; an appropriate balance of love, work, and leisure pursuits."

According to WHO (World Health Organization), mental health is:

> "a state of well-being in which the individual realizes his or her own abilities, can cope with the normal stresses of life, can work productively and fruitfully, and is able to make a contribution to his or her community". WHO stresses that mental health "is not just the absence of mental disorder."

WHO explains that especially in low- and middle-income countries, mental health services are very underfunded - both human and financial. Most resources are channelled into treating and caring for mentally ill patients, rather than on any integrated mental health system. Countries should integrate mental health into primary health care (general practice), provide mental health care in general hospitals, and improve community-based mental health services, rather than just providing care in large psychiatric hospitals.

Mental Health Problems (disorders) can affect anyone

Experts say we all have the potential for suffering from mental health problems, no matter how old we are, whether we are male or female, rich or poor, or ethnic group we belong to. In the UK over one quarter of a million people are admitted into psychiatric hospitals each year, and more than 4,000 people kill themselves. Thcy come from all walks of life.

According to the NIMH (National Institute of Mental Health, USA) mental disorders are "common in the USA and internationally". Approximately 57.7 million Americans suffer from a mental disorder in a given year, that is approximately 26.2% of adults. However, the main burden of illness is concentrated in about 1 in 17 people (6%) who suffer from a serious mental illness. Approximately half of all people who suffer from a mental disorder probably suffer from another mental disorder at the same time, experts say.

In the UK, Canada, the USA and much of the developed world, mental disorders are the leading cause of disability among people aged 15 to 44.

What are—mental illness, mental disorders and mental health problems?

Mental illness is a term that is used to refer to a wide range of mental disorders that can be diagnosed by a health care professional. *In this chapter, mental illness, mental disorders and mental health problems have the same meaning.*

Mental Illnesses

The most common forms of mental illnesses are:

- **Anxiety disorders**—the most common group of mental illnesses. The sufferer has a severe fear or anxiety which is linked to certain objects or situations. Most people with an anxiety disorder will try to avoid exposure to whatever triggers their anxiety. Examples of anxiety disorders include:

— **Panic disorder**—the person experiences sudden paralyzing terror or imminent disaster.

— **Phobias**—these may include *simple phobias* - disproportionate fear of objects, *social phobias* - fear of being subject to the judgment of others, and *agoraphobia* - dread of situations where getting away or breaking free may be difficult. We really do not know how many phobias people may experience globally - there could be hundreds and hundreds of them.

— **(OCD) Obsessive-compulsive disorder**—the person has obsessions and compulsions. In other words, constant stressful thoughts (obsessions), and a powerful urge to perform repetitive acts, such as hand washing (compulsion).

— **PSTD (Post-traumatic stress disorder)**—this can occur after somebody has been through a traumatic event - something horrible and scary that the person sees or that happens to them. During this type of event the person thinks that his/her life or other people's lives are in danger. The sufferer may feel afraid or feel that he/she has no control over what is happening.

- **Mood disorders** - these are also known as affective disorders or depressive disorders. Patients with these illnesses share disturbances or mood changes, generally involving either mania (elation) or depression. Experts say that approximately 80% of patients with depressive disorder improve significantly with treatment. Examples of mood disorders include:

— **Major depression** - the sufferer is not longer interested in and does not enjoy activities and events that he/she previously got pleasure from. There are extreme or prolonged periods of sadness.

— **Bipolar disorder** - also known as manic-depressive illness, or manic depression. The sufferer oscillates from episodes of euphoria (mania) and depression (despair).

— **Dysthymia** - mild chronic depression. Chronic in medicine means continuous and long-term. The patient has a chronic feeling of ill being and/or lack of interest in activities he/she once enjoyed - but to a lesser extent than in major depression.

— **SAD (seasonal affective disorder)** - a type of major depression. However, this one is triggered by lack of daylight. People get it in countries far from the equator during late autumn, winter, and early spring.

- **Schizophrenia disorders**—Whether or not schizophrenia is a single disorder or a group of related illnesses has yet to be fully determined. It is a highly complex illness, with some generalizations which exist in virtually all patients diagnosed with schizophrenia disorders. Most sufferers experience onset of schizophrenia between 15 and 25 years of age. The sufferer has thoughts that appear fragmented; he/she also finds it hard to process information. Schizophrenia can have *negative* or *positive* symptoms. Positive symptoms include delusions, thought disorders and hallucinations. Negative symptoms include withdrawal, lack of motivation and a flat or inappropriate mood.

Serious Mental Disorders/illnesses

Most major (serious) mental illnesses tend to have symptoms that come and go, with periods in between when the person can lead a relatively normal life (episodic illness). The most common serious mental disorders are:

- Schizophrenia
- Bipolar disorder
- Depression

Treatments and Strategies for mental health problems

There are various ways people with mental health problems might receive treatment. It is important to know that what works for one person may not work for another; this is especially the case with mental health. Some strategies or treatment are more successful when combined with others. The patient himself/herself with a chronic (long-term) mental disorder may draw on different options at different stages in his/her life. The majority of experts say that the well informed patient is probably the best judge of what treatment suits him/her better. It is crucial that healthcare professionals be aware of this.

Self help

There are a lot people with mental health problems may do to improve their mental health. Alterations in lifestyle, which may include a better diet, lower alcohol and illegal drug consumption, exercise and getting enough sleep can make enormous differences to a mental health patient's mental health. Let's have a closer look and some of these strategies:

Diet and Mental Health

Scientists, psychiatrists, and other health care professionals know that the brain is made up in large part of essential fatty acids, water and other nutrients. It is an accepted fact that food affects how people feel, think and behave. Most experts accept that dietary interventions could have an impact on a number of the mental health challenges society faces today. So, why is it that governments and public health authorities in developed economies invest so little in developing this knowledge? The evidence is growing and becoming more compelling that diet can play a significant role in the care and treatment of people with mental health problems, including depression, ADHD (attention deficit hyperactivity disorder) to name but a few. If experts are talking about an integrated approach which recognizes the interplay of biological, psychological, social and environmental factors - with diet in the middle of it as being key - and challenging the growing burden of mental health problems in developed nations, surely individuals can speed things up and do something about their diet themselves and improve their mental health.

- It is estimated that in the UK people eat four kilograms of food additives each year. We are not sure what effect decades of such consumption may have on the brain. We don't know for one simple reason - governments are reluctant to fund, conduct or publish rigorously controlled large scale studies which look at the effect of additives on human mental health.

  Changing farming practices have introduced higher levels of different types of fat into our diet. For example, chickens reach their ideal weight for slaughter twice as quickly today compared to three decades ago - this has changed the nutritional profile of meat, according to a report by the Mental Health Foundation (UK). Three decades ago a typical chicken carcass used to be 2% fat - today they are a whopping 22%. The omega-3 fatty acid content in chicken meat has dropped while the omega-6 fatty acids have risen. The same is happening to farmed fish.

- The function of fats and amino acids in our brains:

  Our brains' *dry weight* consists of approximately 60 per cent fat. Our brain cell membranes are directly affected by the fats we eat. Saturated fats make our brain cell membranes less flexible. Saturated fats are those that harden at room temperature.Twenty per cent of the fat that exists in our brain is made up of essential fatty acids omega-3 and omega-6. The word *essential* here means we cannot make it ourselves, so we have to consume it in order to get it.

  Fatty acids perform crucial functions in the structuring of neurons (brain cells), making sure that optimal communication is maintained within the brain. Nutritionists say omega-3 and omega-6 essential fatty acids should be consumed in equal amounts. If we consume unequal amounts there is a higher chance of having problems with depression, concentration and memory. It is crucial omega-3 intake is kept up. While one study shows a link between omega-3 intake and mental skills, others show there are benefits for cardiovascular problems, diabetes, ADHD, and a host of other problems:

Experts recommend that infant formula should include DHA omega-3 and AA omega-6 to guarantee correct eye and brain development. The diet of Typical North Americans is deficient in omega-3 fatty acids and may pose a risk to infant development.

Trans-fat, which has appeared in growing quantities into much of the food we eat over the last few decades, assumes the same position as essential fatty acids in the brain. In other words, the proper vital nutrients are not able to assume their right position for the brain to function effectively. Trans-fats are commonly found in cakes, biscuits, shortbread, some pastries and many ready meals.

Neurotransmitters, such as serotonin, are made from amino acids which we often have to get by eating it. If you want to feed your brain with good stuff eat less intensively farmed chicken and meat, and go for organic chicken and non-farmed oily fish, such as tuna, sardines, trout, or salmon.

The Mental Health Foundation has a booklet *"Healthy eating and depression"*, for anyone who wishes to protect their mental health through healthy eating. A study found that eating a Mediterranean diet appears to be associated with less risk of mild cognitive impairment - a stage between normal aging and dementia or of transitioning from mild cognitive impairment into Alzheimer's disease.

An Australian study found that a high quality breakfast, with foods from at least three different healthy food groups, was linked with better mental health in 14 year old boys and girls. The researchers found that for every extra food group eaten at breakfast, the associated mental health score improved.

- **Exercise and Mental Health**

  An interesting animal study found that physical and mental exercises help improve schizophrenia symptoms.

  A Harvard University study found that exercise may help people with depression by enhancing body image, providing social support from exercise groups, a distraction for every day worries, heightened self-confidence from meeting a goal, and altered circulation of the neurotransmitters serotonin, norepinephrine, and the endorphins.

  Even a very small amount of additional exercise has been seen to have an important impact on mental health. A Scottish study involving 20,000 people found that performing as little as twenty minutes of any physical activity, including housework, per week is enough to boost mental health.

- Exercise can boost an exercise-related gene in the brain that works as a powerful anti-depressant, scientists at the Yale School of Medicine found. They then compared the brain activity of sedentary mice to those who were given running wheels. The researchers observed that the mice with wheels within one week were running more than six miles each night. Four independent array analyses of the mice turned up 33 hippocampal exercise-regulated genes-27 of which had never been identified before.

The UK's National Institute for Clinical Excellence (NICE) issued guidelines for health professionals on how to encourage older people to engage in more physical activity as a way to boost their mental health; one suggestion is for GPs to encourage their older patients to join local walking schemes and tell them how walking benefits mental wellbeing.

Another study, carried out in the United Kingdom found that regular intense physical exercise is linked with lower rates of depression and anxiety in men up to five years later.

Sadly, the Mental Health Foundation found that very few UK patients are offered the choice of exercise therapy for mild to moderate depression. Apparently, only 5% of GPs (general practitioners, primary care physicians) use it as one of their most regular treatment responses, compared to 92% who use antidepressants as one of their most popular treatment responses. In 2006 only 42% of UK GPs reported having access to exercise referral schemes, despite the overwhelming evidence of its benefits for patients. Even among GPs who do have access to exercise referral schemes, only 15% use them very frequently or frequently for patients with mild or moderate depression. Unfortunately, apart from a couple of exceptions, much of the rest of the world's health care professionals seem to ignore exercise as a vital treatment for mental illness.

If you have a mental disorder, remember that you can do the exercise yourself. You do not need to wait for your doctor to "prescribe" it for you. Perhaps you should initially check whether you are in acceptable physical health to do exercise. If you are not, insist that your doctor help you devise an exercise plan that suits you. The benefits may surprise you.

Alcohol is a Common form of "Self-medication" for people with Mental Health Problems

There is evidence that very moderate alcohol consumption may aid mental health in some cases. However, the evidence is overwhelming that excessive alcohol has a very bad impact on people's mental health. Whatever your attitude is to alcohol, remember that alcohol will not resolve your mental health problems, and will most likely make them worse if you are not very, very careful.

Drinking to deal with difficult feelings or symptoms is referred to by some mental health professionals as *self medication*. It is important to know that excessive drinking is a likely medium to long term consequence of this type of self medication. Most studies clearly prove that consuming high amounts expose people to significant risks of higher levels of mental health problems. People who suffer from more severe mental health problems are more likely to have alcohol problems too, compared to other people. Experts say this does not necessarily mean that alcohol causes severe mental illness. Perhaps it is more linked to 'self-medication'.

A report in 2008 said that urgent action is needed to prevent a 'silent epidemic' of alcohol-related dementia in the UK.

A statistical modeling study suggests that problems with alcohol abuse may lead to an increased risk of depression, as opposed to the reverse model in which individuals with depression self-medicate with alcohol. In other words, alcohol increases depression risk - it is not the other way round.

A study found a clear link between binge drinking and depression. It seems the link is stronger for women. However, the relationship between alcohol use and depression when depression is measured as recent feeling of depressions or unhappiness, is the same for both sexes.

Scientists at the University of North Carolina School of medicine found that stopping drinking - including at moderate levels - may lead to health problems including depression and a reduced capacity of the brain to produce new neurons, a process called neurogenesis.

World Mental Health Day: 10 October

World Mental Health Day on 10 October raises public awareness about mental health issues. The Day promotes more open discussion of mental disorders, and investments in prevention and treatment services. The treatment gap for mental, neurological and substance use disorders is formidable especially in poor resource countries. On the occasion of the World Mental Health Day, WHO is launching its Mental Health Gap Intervention Guide.

Suicide Prevention

Magnitude of the Problem

Suicide is among the top 20 leading causes of death globally for all ages. Every year, nearly one million people die from suicide.

Risk Factors

Mental illness, primarily depression and alcohol use disorders, abuse, violence, loss, cultural and social background, represent major risk factors for suicide.

Prevention

Restriction of access to means of suicide, such as toxic substances and firearms, identification and management of persons suffering from mental and substance use disorders, improved access to health and social services, and responsible reporting of suicide by the media are effective strategies for the prevention of suicide.

Suicide prevention (SUPRE)

The Problem

- Every year, almost one million people die from suicide; a "global" mortality rate of 16 per 100,000, or one death every 40 seconds.

- In the past 45 years suicide rates have increased by 60% worldwide. Suicide is among the three leading causes of death among those aged 15-44 years in some countries, and the second leading cause of death in the 10-24 years age group; these figures do not include suicide attempts which are up to 20 times more frequent than completed suicide.
- Suicide worldwide is estimated to represent 1.8% of the total global burden of disease in 1998, and 2.4% in countries with market and former socialist economies in 2020.
- Although traditionally suicide rates have been highest among the male elderly, rates among young people have been increasing to such an extent that they are now the group at highest risk in a third of countries, in both developed and developing countries.

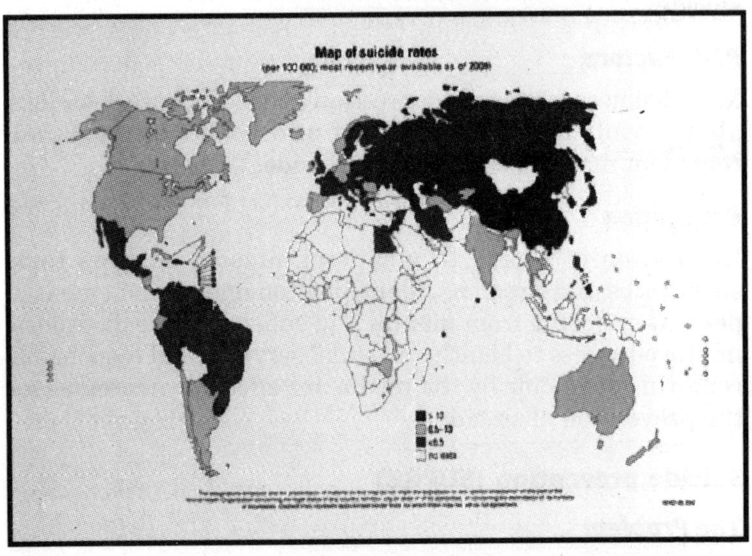

Suicide statistics

Source : Country reports and charts available & Global charts

- Mental disorders (particularly depression and alcohol use disorders) are a major risk factor for suicide in Europe and North America; however, in Asian countries impulsiveness plays an important role. Suicide is complex with psychological, social, biological, cultural and environmental factors involved.

Suicide Statistics

Effective Interventions

- Strategies involving restriction of access to common methods of suicide, such as firearms or toxic substances like pesticides, have proved to be effective in reducing suicide rates; however, there is a need to adopt multi-sectoral approaches involving many levels of intervention and activities.
- There is compelling evidence indicating that adequate prevention and treatment of depression and alcohol and substance abuse can reduce suicide rates, as well as follow-up contact with those who have attempted suicide.

Challenges and Obstacles

- Worldwide, the prevention of suicide has not been adequately addressed due to basically a lack of awareness of suicide as a major problem and the taboo in many societies to discuss openly about it. In fact, only a few countries have included prevention of suicide among their priorities.
- Reliability of suicide certification and reporting is an issue in great need of improvement.
- It is clear that suicide prevention requires intervention also from outside the health sector and calls for an innovative, comprehensive multi-sectoral approach, including both health and non-health sectors, e.g. education, labour, police, justice, religion, law, politics, the media.

Maternal Mental Health and Child Health and Development

The Issue

Maternal mental health problems pose a huge human, social and economic burden to women, their infants, their families, and society and constitute a major public health challenge. Although the overall prevalence of mental disorders is similar in men and women, women's mental health requires special considerations in view of women's greater likelihood of suffering from depression and anxiety disorders and the impact of mental health problems on child-bearing and child-rearing, too:

- Depression and anxiety are approximately twice as prevalent globally in women as in men, and are at their highest rates in the lifecycle during the childbearing years, from puberty to menopause.
- Studies of depression and anxiety show their incidence to be approximately 5% in non-pregnant women, approximately 8-10% during pregnancy and highest (13%) in the year following delivery.
- Suicide is one of the most common causes of maternal death in the year following delivery in developed countries.
- Psychosis, by contrast, is relatively rare and occurs in only 1 to 2 women for every 1000 giving birth. The rates of psychosis following delivery may be higher in less developed countries, where infection may contribute to its occurrence.

Who is at Risk of these Disorders?

Virtually all women can develop mental disorders during pregnancy and in the first year after delivery, but poverty, migration, extreme stress, exposure to violence (domestic, sexual and gender-based), emergency and conflict situations, natural disasters, and low social support generally increase risks for specific disorders.

Consequences of Maternal Mental Disorders during Pregnancy

During pregnancy the affected woman is less likely to eat and sleep well and may fail to adequately gain weight. She is less likely to attend prenatal care and may even fail to seek help for the birth. She is more likely to use harmful substances such as alcohol, cigarettes and drugs and may attempt to injure or kill herself.

Stress hormones are raised during maternal mental illness and may have also has physical effects on the mother (predisposing her to maternal high blood pressure, pre-eclampsia, early and difficult delivery) and on the developing babies, who may be and small for age infants.

Effects of Maternal Mental Disorders after Birth on the Mother, Infant and Family

After the birth, the depressed mother may fail to adequately eat, bathe or care for herself in other ways. This may increase the risks of infection and anaemia. The risk of suicide is also a consideration, and in psychotic illnesses, the risk of infanticide must also be considered.

Very young infants can be affected by and are highly sensitive to the environment (largely represented by the mother) and the quality of care, and are likely to be affected by mothers with mental disorders – especially if the mother has low mood, social withdrawal, irritability, impaired thinking and feelings of hopelessness.

Prolonged or severe mental illness hampers the mother-infant attachment, breastfeeding and infant care. Depressed and anxious mothers are less likely to look at their infants' faces and emotionally connect with them, and they are also less likely to understand cues of hunger, happiness or distress and therefore are less responsive to the baby.

- Infants of chronically depressed mothers show less sociability with strangers, fewer facial expressions, smile less, cry more, and are more irritable than infants of normal mothers.

- Children of chronically depressed mothers do not perform as well on thinking and intelligence tests at 18 months of age and this is especially true for boy babies' speech development.
- Children of depressed mothers are also more distractible, less playful and less social up to age 5.

The effects of maternal mental disorder in older children in the family may include neglect, abuse and slower social, emotional and cognitive development, including higher rates of school and behaviour problems.

Maternal mental illness may have serious effects also on the marital relationships, especially in the case of prolonged or serious mental disorder. These may include disruption of the marriage and/or spousal abuse by either partner.

Steps to be taken

Although in many settings different levels of mental health care continues to be provided in isolation from general health care, we know now that it can be integrated into general health care; this is also valid for maternal mental health care.

Prevention

The most common preventive strategy has been to modify risk factors for maternal mental disorders. Numerous studies have evaluated preventive interventions including social support, as well as educational, psychological and pharmacologic models of care; other interventions, such as exercise, massage, herbs and rituals have also been used.

Identification of maternal mental disorders

Simple questions asked during pregnancy and in the postpartum period may help to identify women at greater risk for mental disorders, for instance:

- Depression: "How much of the time during the last month have you felt down hearted and blue?";

- Anxiety: "How much of the time during the last month have you been a very nervous person?";
- Psychosis: "Have you been receiving any special messages from people or from the way things are arranged around you?"

Management and Care

- The hopeful message is that 70-80% of women with maternal mental disorders can be successfully treated and recover! This is good news for the woman, her infant and her family! The woman and her partner, if appropriate, should be involved in education about maternal mental disorders, treatment and decision-making.
- Another positive message is that to a large extent the identification and management of most of these mental disorders can be done at primary health care level, by first line interveners, incorporated into primary health care routines.

Women who self-identify as distressed, or who are identified through healthcare workers, family, friends, or screening, as possibly suffering from a maternal mental disorder need a timely contact with trained first-level care providers. The healthcare system must also facilitate the referral of these women to trained mental health professionals, whenever needed.

Education about maternal mental health should be part of all health disciplines' training, including in-service training. National or state governments need to make these issues a priority for education and provision of adequate services through financial resources targeted towards pregnant and postpartum women with mental disorders, and their infants and children.

CHILD AND ADOLESCENT MENTAL HEALTH

Child and Adolescent Mental Health Initiatives of the Department of Mental Health and Substance Abuse

For the past two years the Department has supported the development of a coordinated child and adolescent mental health programme. The programme has fostered a recognition throughout WHO and in the WHO Regions that child and adolescent mental health is a necessary priority for the healthy development of societies. Child and adolescent mental health is central to the future development of low income countries throughout the world, but in particular in sub-Saharan Africa and elsewhere where AIDS orphans, displaced populations of child combatants, reintegrated child soldiers, AIDS affected and infected youth and youth marginalized because of lack of economic opportunity are jeopardizing the future of whole nations. Furthermore, the free and forced migration from Africa and other parts of the world affected by conflict brings to the shores of the United States and elsewhere youth who are unable to integrate into society because of mental health problems. The economic and social consequences are obvious and now well documented. WHO has developed initiatives that will address these core problems at their origin and provide programmatic support.

WHO's Department of Mental Health and Substance Abuse has initiated three programmes which together form a coordinated effort to address global child and adolescent mental health problems. The programme at its very core appreciates the global interdependence of societies. The three programme elements include (1) a campaign on the stigma associated with mental illness among youth, (2) a global policy initiative that will equip ministries of health to develop coordinated, responsive programmes where child and adolescent mental health will be integrated into overall health care, and (3) a programme to assess the global treatment gap associated with mental illness. In regard to all of these programmes there is a keen awareness that poor mental health on the part of youth leads to lack of compliance with medical regimens, participation in health promotion activities, failure to achieve educationally, lack of ability to participate in work skills development, and adds to the burden in developing societies with increased participation and instigation of violence, abuse of self and others, and support for a broad range of illegal activities. The activities related to identifying treatment resources and the policy initiative parallel the original programmes addressing adult mental health issues.

The World Health Day 2001 featured a school contest for children and adolescents around the world addressing the problem of stigma. The theme of the contest mirrored the theme of World Health Day "Dare to Care: Stop Exclusion." The contest drew worldwide participation and has resulted in the publication of a WHO book "Through Children's Eyes" which provides, through essays and pictures, a child and adolescent view of stigma associated with mental disorders. The book also contains brief descriptions of several mental disorders prominent in youth and a guide for teachers to help lead discussions with youth about stigma. The goal is to see this product lead to a broader campaign on reducing stigma associated with child and adolescent mental disorders. In the future, we visualize a series of regional meetings on stigma followed by a coordinated series of training for a broad range of community resources including religious leaders, educators, key community leaders and parents. In addition, we will develop an enhanced curriculum on mental disorders for use with youth in health education programmes throughout the world. The anti-stigma campaign will be linked to the ongoing policy initiative.

The child and adolescent mental health policy initiative seeks to provide countries with the tools to develop appropriate, sustainable mental health policy. A particular focus is on the stewardship of resources, both human and financial. The child and adolescent component of this broader WHO mental health policy initiative requires a considerable extra effort since international surveys have found a dearth of existing policy. Regional development meetings, key country technical assistance and the dissemination of information to NGOs, governmental organizations will follow on finalization of the policy and services guidance document.

Lastly, the child and adolescent ATLAS resources survey will provide important baseline data to complete the development of policy at the national level. The survey, which has already been initiated, will be the first of its kind and will provide a key tool for interacting with policymakers in countries and with those who seek to develop more coordinated and cost-effective services. In the future WHO will hold technical workshops to demonstrate the use of the epidemiological and demographic data for key countries, again focusing on low-income countries.

In addition to the focused programme areas, the Department has recently sponsored a conference on "Caring for Children and Adolescents with Mental Disorders: Setting the WHO Agenda." This meeting brought together experts from the WHO Regions to discuss issues related to diagnosis and treatment. Gaps in knowledge, issues related to clinical practice and policy considerations were explored. The Report of the meeting was recently published and is available on request. An electronic version can be accessed on line in the Publications. During the coming year it will be made available in several languages.

The child and adolescent mental health programme serves as an internal resource to other WHO programmes involved with child and adolescent health and more targeted initiatives. Statements on particular aspects of practice will be forthcoming as a result of consultations with the WHO Regions. The child and adolescent mental health programme also responds to public inquiries.

GENDER AND WOMEN'S MENTAL HEALTH

Gender disparities and mental health: The Facts

Mental illness is associated with a significant burden of morbidity and disability.

Lifetime prevalence rates for any kind of psychological disorder are higher than previously thought, are increasing in recent cohorts and affect nearly half the population.

Despite being common, mental illness is underdiagnosed by doctors. Less than half of those who meet diagnostic criteria for psychological disorders are identified by doctors.

Patients, too, appear reluctant to seek professional help. Only 2 in every 5 people experiencing a mood, anxiety or substance use disorder seeking assistance in the year of the onset of the disorder.

Overall rates of psychiatric disorder are almost identical for men and women but striking gender differences are found in the patterns of mental illness.

Why Gender?

Gender is a critical determinant of mental health and mental illness. The morbidity associated with mental illness has received substantially more attention than the gender specific determinants and mechanisms that promote and protect mental health and foster resilience to stress and adversity.

Gender determines the differential power and control men and women have over the socioeconomic determinants of their mental health and lives, their social position, status and treatment in society and their susceptibility and exposure to specific mental health risks.

Gender differences occur particularly in the rates of common mental disorders - depression, anxiety and somatic complaints. These disorders, in which women predominate, affect approximately 1 in 3 people in the community and constitute a serious public health problem.

Unipolar depression, predicted to be the second leading cause of global disability burden by 2020, is twice as common in women.

Depression is not only the most common women's mental health problem but may be more persistent in women than men. More research is needed.

Reducing the overrepresentation of women who are depressed would contribute significantly to lessening the global burden of disability caused by psychological disorders.

The lifetime prevalence rate for alcohol dependence, another common disorder, is more than twice as high in men than women. In developed countries, approximately 1 in 5 men and 1 in 12 women develop alcohol dependence during their lives.

Men are also more than three times more likely to be diagnosed with antisocial personality disorder than women.

There are no marked gender differences in the rates of severe mental disorders like schizophrenia and bipolar disorder that affect less than 2% of the population.

Gender differences have been reported in age of onset of symptoms, frequency of psychotic symptoms, course of these disorders, social adjustment and long term outcome.

The disability associated with mental illness falls most heavily on those who experience three or more comorbid disorders. Again, women predominate.

Gender Specific Risk Factors

Depression, anxiety, somatic symptoms and high rates of comorbidity are significantly related to interconnected and co-occurrent risk factors such as gender based roles, stressors and negative life experiences and events.

Gender specific risk factors for common mental disorders that disproportionately affect women include gender based violence, socioeconomic disadvantage, low income and income inequality, low or subordinate social status and rank and unremitting responsibility for the care of others.

The high prevalence of sexual violence to which women are exposed and the correspondingly high rate of Post Traumatic Stress Disorder (PTSD) following such violence, renders women the largest single group of people affected by this disorder.

The mental health impact of long term, cumulative psychosocial adversity has not been adequately investigated.

Restructuring has a gender specific effect on mental health.

Economic and social policies that cause sudden, disruptive and severe changes to income, employment and social capital that cannot be controlled or avoided, significantly increase gender inequality and the rate of common mental disorders.

Gender Bias

Gender bias occurs in the treatment of psychological disorders. Doctors are more likely to diagnose depression in women compared with men, even when they have similar scores on standardized measures of depression or present with identical symptoms.

Female gender is a significant predictor of being prescribed mood altering psychotropic drugs.

Gender differences exist in patterns of help seeking for psychological disorder. Women are more likely to seek help from and disclose mental health problems to their primary health care physician while men are more likely to seek specialist mental health care and are the principal users of inpatient care.

Men are more likely than women to disclose problems with alcohol use to their health care provider.

Gender stereotypes regarding proneness to emotional problems in women and alcohol problems in men, appear to reinforce social stigma and constrain help seeking along stereotypical lines. They are a barrier to the accurate identification and treatment of psychological disorder.

Despite these differences, most women and men experiencing emotional distress and /or psychological disorder are neither identified or treated by their doctor.

Violence related mental health problems are also poorly identified. Women are reluctant to disclose a history of violent victimization unless physicians ask about it directly.

The complexity of violence related health outcomes increases when victimization is undetected and results in high and costly rates of utilization of the health and mental health care system.

MENTAL HEALTH AND PSYCHOSOCIAL SUPPORT IN EMERGENCIES

General Information related to most Emergencies

The target group for WHO work on mental health and psychosocial support in emergencies is any population exposed to extreme stressors, such as refugees, internally displaced persons, disaster survivors and terrorism-, war- or genocide-exposed populations. The WHO Department of Mental Health and Substance Abuse emphasizes that the number of persons exposed to extreme stressors is large and that exposure to extreme stressors is a risk factor for mental health and social problems. The Department's work on mental health in emergencies focuses mostly on resource-poor countries, where most populations exposed to natural disasters and war live.

The Department's objectives, with respect to the mental and social aspects of health of populations exposed to extreme stressors are:

- to be a resource in terms of technical advice for policy and field activities by governmental, nongovernmental and intergovernmental organizations;

- to provide leadership and guidance to improve policy and interventions in the field;
- to facilitate the generation of an evidence base for field activities and policy at community and health system level.

Important is Mental Health

Mental health has a huge impact on every aspect of your life.

• *Self-image*

Good mental health means appreciating your achievements and accepting your shortcomings. A mental illness can cause an inferiority complex, a negative body image, and intense feelings of self-hate, anger, disgust, and uselessness, which could mutate into extreme depression, psycho-social disorders, or eating disorders.

• *Education*

Students with mental problems socially isolate themselves, and develop anxiety disorders and concentration problems. Good mental health ensures an all-round educational experience that enhances social and intellectual skills that lead to self-confidence and better grades.

• *Relationships*

Mental health largely contributes to the functioning of human relationships. Mental illness can hamper even basic interactions with family, friends, and colleagues. Most people suffering from mental illness find it difficult to nurture relationships, have problems with commitment or intimacy, and frequently encounter sexual health issues.

• *Sleep*

An inability to handle stress or anxiety can cause insomnia. Even if you mange to fall asleep, you may wake up a dozen times during the night with thoughts of what went wrong the day before or how bad tomorrow is going to be. You may develop severe sleeping disorders which leave you exhausted and less productive.

- ***Eating***

People with mental disorders are more prone to indulging in comfort eating or emotional binges. Finding comfort in food is something we all do from time to time. But with a mental illness, it becomes difficult to control yourself. Overeating can lead to obesity, which puts you at a risk for heart disease and diabetes, in addition to creating an unhealthy body-image.

- ***Physical Health***

Your mental state directly affects your body. For example, stress can lead to hypertension or stomach ulcers. People who are mentally healthy are at a lower risk for many health complications.

So make a conscious effort to improve and maintain your mental health.

Good health is not a struggle, nor it is an extraordinary feat. Healthy living is about understanding what your body needs and what is good for it. Re-discover good health in a simple way with Tania Hackner and make good health a way of living!

REFERENCES

Christian Nordqvist, Copyright: Medical News Today, www.medicalnewstoday.com/articles/154543.php

http://www.who.int/mental_health/en/

http://www.who.int/mental_health/prevention

http://www.who.int/mental_health/emergencies

http://www.medicinalnews.com

CHAPTER

11

Responsible Causes of Female Foeticide (A Sociological Study of Agra City)

— Dr. Bandana Gaur

Female Foeticide refers to the sex-selective abortion, i.e. the Female child is being killed in the womb. The term Foeticide means, abortion of the foetus deliberately. According to Kamla Munneker "It is murder in advance of a women". For business minded doctors, it is a normal phenomenon. The parents do not also see only fault in it. But it is reality that female foetus abortion is a murder of a girl committed by the couple and doctor deliberately.

Objectives of the Study

- To know why there is inferiority complex in having a girl child.
- To study the effects of female foeticide on every individual.
- To know why a boy child is preferred over a girl child.
- To study who is the responsible for the female foeticide.

Hypotheses

- In male dominated society, female considered an inferior species in our social sphere.

- Orthodox nature and double standard in our society.
- One of the strong reasons is dowry and ignorance.
- Much preference to sex selective technology.

Methodology

The present study is based on primary data collection. It was prepared to select the sample unit by using random sampling method. The sample size restricted to 50 woman respondent. The questionnaire is shaped to know the sociological analysis of responsible causes of Female Foeticide. The data has been collected from the selected area of Agra city at Dayalbagh. A random sampling of 50 women has given the opinion towards female foeticide.

Questionnaire

Following questions were asked to the respondent:-

1. Who is responsible for female foeticide?
2. Is economic occurrence responsible for female foeticide?
3. Is it necessary that the son is only responsible for religious rituals?
4. Is female foeticide helpful for family planning?
5. Is the government aware for female foeticide?

Table 11.1 : Age-wise Data Analysis

Age Group	No. of Respondent	Percentage
20-30	21	42
30-40	15	30
40-50	10	20
50 lavel	04	08
Total	**50**	**100**

Table 11.2 : Education Qualification

Age Group	No. of Respondent	Percentage
Below intermediate	03	06
Intermediate	06	12
UG	18	36
PG	23	46
Total	**50**	**100**

Table 11.3 : Religion-wise Classification

Age Group	No. of Respondent	Percentage
Hindu	18	36
Sikh	20	40
Jain	08	16
Christian	04	08
Total	**50**	**100**

Table 11.4 : Main Reason for Female Foeticide

Age Group	No. of Respondent	Percentage
Literacy	07	14
Orthodoxy	26	52
Technology	17	34
Total	**50**	**100**

Table 11.5 : Son is Responsible for Religious Rituals

Age Group	No. of Respondent	Percentage
Yes	32	64
No	18	36
Total	**50**	**100**

Table 11.6 : Economic Causes Responsible for Female Foeticide

Age Group	No. of Respondent	Percentage
Yes	40	80
No	10	20
Total	**50**	**100**

Table 11.7 : Is Female Foeticide Helpful for Family Planning?

Age Group	No. of Respondent	Percentage
Yes	22	44
No	28	56
Total	**50**	**100**

Table 11.8 : Who is the Responsible for Female Foeticide?

Age Group	No. of Respondent	Percentage
Doctors	06	12
Scan-Machine	14	28
Individual	30	60
Total	**50**	**100**

Table 11.9 : Is the Government aware for Female Foeticide

Age Group	No. of Respondent	Percentage
Yes	39	78
No	11	22
Total	**50**	**100**

Data Analysis

Among the total respondent out of 50 women, aged between 20-30 and above 50, have given opinion in the present study. From the collected sample of the respondents, 46 percent of the women are at PG level, 36 UG level educated, 12 intermediate level and three per cent below intermediate level have given their views about the Female Foeticide. On the basis of Religion, 40 percent Sikh and 36 per cent Hindu have given opinion on the female Foeticide. From the collected sample of the respondents, 52 per cent of the women agreed that orthodox is the main reason for Female Foeticide. The economic reason wise data shows that 80 per cent women accepted that the economic causes are responsible for the female foeticide. Among the total respondents, 64 per cent women have agreed that the son preference is responsible for religious rituals. 44 per cent women have given opinion that the female Foeticide is helpful for family planning while the 56 per cent disagreed. From the collected sample of the respondent 60 per cent that the individual are the responsible for female foeticide. 78 per cent women agreed that the government is aware for female foeticide and 22 per cent disagreed with this opinion.

Result of the Study

- Fifty-two per cent of women agreed that orthodox is the main reason of Female Foeticide.
- Eighty per cent of women accepted that the economic causes are responsible for female Foeticide.
- Sixty four per cent of women agreed with the reason that son preference is responsible for female foeticide.
- Sixty per cent of women accepted that the individuals are responsible for the female Foeticide.

Suggestion

- Society should provide equal status to both male and female
- No feeling of inferiority complex towards girls.
- Eradication of orthodox and double standards hypocrisy.
- Check and reduction in mushrooming of pre-natal scan centers.
- Effort towards literacy and prohibition of dowry system.

- Reduction in importance of sex selective technology.
- Decline in systematic negligence of girls.
- Adôpt family planning but not through female foeticide.
- Neglect socio-religions factors.
- Avoidance of son preference.
- Women to be considered as responsible part of society not burden on the society.

Conclusion

Female Foeticide is killing the female child in the womb. Reasons for its increase are due to sharp rise in numbers of scan machines, socio-economic cultural discrimination against women, son preference and negligence of girl child. The problem needs to be eradicated at various levels and from all angles. Women must be given security. A comprehensive programme, such as creating awareness among man and woman be launched.

REFERENCES

Saraswati, Dr. Mishra, *Status of Indian Women*, Gyan Publishing House, New Delhi, 2002, p. 247.

Moniker, Kamla, *Abortion; A Social Dilemma,* Vikash Publishing house, New Delhi 1973, p. 2

Mitra, M.S. and Maharana of Baroda, 1984; *The Position of Women in Indian Life.* Neeraj Publishing House, Delhi.

Mourya, S.D. (Ed.) 1988: *Women in India: A demographic profile*, Chugh Publication, Allahabad.

Sriniwas M.N. Chemging status of Indian women.

Times of India (2004), p. 7

Hindu 14th December, 2003, p. 14.

India Today-17 Nov., 2003.

Hindustan Times, 30 Jan. 2002.

Times of India, 23 Dec. 2001.

Index